TIM FLANNERY

EXPLORING THE WORLD'S INCREDIBLE DRYLANDS

WEIRD, WILD, AMAZING!

ART BY
SAM CALDWELL

DESERT

FOR COLEBY AND DANIEL

Text copyright © 2019 by Tim Flannery
Illustrations copyright © 2019 by Sam Caldwell
Design copyright © 2019 by Hardie Grant Egmont

First published in Australia in 2019 by Hardie Grant Egmont as
part of EXPLORE YOUR WORLD: Weird, Wild, Amazing!
Previously published in the US in 2020 as part of WEIRD, WILD, AMAZING!:
Exploring the Incredible World of Animals.

For information about permission to reproduce selections from this book, write to
Permissions, W. W. Norton & Company, Inc., 500 Fifth Avenue, New York, NY 10110

For information about special discounts for bulk purchases, please contact
W. W. Norton Special Sales at specialsales@wwnorton.com or 800-233-4830

Manufacturing by TransContinental

ISBN 978-1-324-01949-7 (pbk.)

W. W. Norton & Company, Inc., 500 Fifth Avenue, New York, N.Y. 10110
www.wwnorton.com

W. W. Norton & Company Ltd., 15 Carlisle Street, London W1D 3BS

2 4 6 8 0 9 7 5 3 1

TIM FLANNERY

EXPLORING THE WORLD'S INCREDIBLE DRYLANDS

WEIRD, WILD, AMAZING!

ART BY
SAM CALDWELL

DESERT

Norton Young Readers

An Imprint of W. W. Norton & Company
Independent Publishers Since 1923

INTRODUCTION

I've been interested in animals and fossils for as long as I can remember. I grew up in the suburbs of Melbourne, Victoria, Australia, and there weren't a lot of opportunities near my home to see cool creatures. But when I was eight years old, I was walking on a sandbank at low tide and saw a strange rock. It had markings on it, and I suspected it was something special. I took it to the museum, where a man in a white coat brought me to a hall filled with gray steel cabinets. The man opened one, pulled out a drawer, and lifted out a rock identical to mine. "It's *Lovenia forbesi*," he told me, "the fossilized remains of an extinct sea urchin. They are quite common in the rocks near my home." It was, he thought, about 10 million years old. I was awestruck. Then he asked, "Are you interested in dinosaurs?"

The man put the fossilized sea urchin back, closed the drawer, and opened another. "Hold out your hand," he said, as he placed an odd pointed rock on it. "This is the Cape Paterson Claw. It's a claw from the foot of a dinosaur, and it is the only dinosaur bone ever found in Victoria."

I held the Cape Paterson Claw! I was so excited that I could hardly speak. Learning about fossils led to a big breakthrough for me, and in the months and years that followed I would snorkel and scuba-dive in the bay near where I found that first fossilized sea urchin. I remember one winter afternoon, I spied a length of fossil whale jaw, nearly as long as me, lying on the bottom. Another day, I chanced upon the tooth of a megalodon shark lying in the shallows.

As I grew up, I went further and further afield, into the Australian desert and Great Barrier Reef, where I encountered water-holding frogs, red kangaroos, and magnificent coral. I became a mammologist—someone who studies living mammals. For 20 years I was the curator of mammals at the Australian Museum in Sydney. I visited most of the islands between eastern Indonesia and Fiji, discovering new species of marsupials, rats, and bats. By the time I left the job I'd been on 26 expeditions into the islands north of Australia and discovered more than 30 new living mammal species.

I WAS MORE THAN INTERESTED. I WAS OBSESSED.

If you're interested in animals and nature, you can volunteer at a museum or on a dig, participate in a citizen science program like the Great Backyard Bird Count, or just start your own studies in a local tide pool or pond. If you decide to do a study by yourself, you need to take careful notes and send them to an expert in a museum or university to check them.

If you don't live near a beach, you can study nature in a local park or backyard. The soil and plants will be filled with living things, including birds and insects. But be sure to stay safe as you investigate!

If you're interested in fossils, keep your eyes on the rocks. Look out for curious shapes. And if you do find something, photograph it, or if it is small and portable, take it to your local museum. Most have services to help identify it.

When I was very young I often wished that I had a fun book that would tell me about the weirdest creatures on Earth. That's what I've tried to create here, for you. I hope that you find reading it to be a great adventure in itself, and that it leaves you wanting to see more of the wonderful and mysterious world around us.

Tim Flannery

EVOLUTION

Evolution is a word that describes how animals and plants change over generations. Each generation of living things is made up of individuals that differ a little from each other: some might be bigger, or more brightly colored, for example. And in nature, more animals are born (or germinate, if they're plants) than the environment can support. This means that the individuals that do best in their environment are most likely to survive. For example, if bigger, brighter animals or plants survive better, with each new generation the population will be made up of bigger, brighter individuals. Over many generations, the changes brought about by this "natural selection" can be so great that new species are created.

CLIMATE CHANGE

Earth's climate is changing because of pollution that humans are putting into the atmosphere. Greenhouse gases like carbon dioxide from burning coal, gas, and oil are causing the ground, oceans, and atmosphere to warm up. This might sound good if you live in a cold place, but many consequences of the warming are bad for living things. For example, warmer conditions mean that less water is available in some places, and creatures living in the warming oceans often have less food and oxygen. As seas rise and rainfall changes, and the atmosphere warms, entire habitats are disappearing, causing species to become threatened or even extinct.

SO SAD.

HABITATS

Habitats include places on land, in water, and even in the air. They are the places where animals live, and they vary greatly all across the world. Deserts are very dry habitats, tundras are very cold ones, while rainforests are very stable ones (with little temperature change, for example, between winter and summer). As animals and plants evolve, they become better adapted to their particular habitat. In the *Weird, Wild, Amazing!* books, habitats are grouped into four very broad categories: water, sky, forest, and desert/grasslands. Within each there are many different habitats—far too many to list.

FOSSILS

Fossils are the remains of plants and animals that lived in the past. The chances of you, or any living thing, becoming a fossil is very small. Maybe one in a billion! The first step toward a fossil being created happens when the remains of a plant or animal are buried in sediment like sand or mud. If the conditions are right, over thousands of years the sediment turns to rock, and the remains become "petrified" (which means turned to rock) or preserved in some other form, like an impression (such as a footprint).

COMMON NAMES v. SCIENTIFIC NAMES

Animals and plants have two kinds of names: a common name and a scientific name. The common name of a species is the name that you generally know them by, and these names can vary in different areas. For example, "wolf" is a common name in English, but wolves are called "lobo" in Spanish, and have many different names in other languages. But the scientific name never varies. This means that by using the scientific name, an English-speaking scientist and a Spanish-speaking scientist can understand each other.

Scientific names have two parts. For wolves, the scientific name is *Canis lupus*. The first part (*Canis*, in this case) is known as the genus name, and it is shared with close relatives. For example, the golden jackal's scientific name—*Canis aureus*—also begins with *Canis*. But the combination of genus and species name is unique. For wolves, the species name (*lupus*) means "wolf" in Latin.

EXTINCTION

Scientists use terms like "vulnerable," "threatened," and "endangered" to describe how likely an organism is to become extinct. Extinction occurs when the last individual of a species dies. If an animal is endangered, it means that very few individuals exist, and that they might soon become extinct. If an animal is threatened, it means that they are likely to become endangered in the future, while an animal being classed as vulnerable means that they are likely to become threatened.

ANIMAL TYPES

Animals and plants are classified according to their evolution. Animals, for example, can be divided into those with backbones (vertebrates) and those without (invertebrates). You can't always tell which group a plant or animal belongs to by just looking at them. Sometimes looks can be misleading! Falcons are related not to eagles or kites, which they resemble, but parrots. Parrots and falcons are classified in a group called "Austroaves," meaning "southern birds," because they originated in the southern hemisphere.

CONSERVATION

Conservation means taking care of nature and all of its plants and animals. Governments help by creating national parks, and fining litterbugs and polluters. Scientists play an important role in conservation by studying how we can help various species. You can be a conservationist in your own backyard: just plant a native tree that will become a home to the birds.

CONSERVE TO PRESERVE!

DESERT
& GRASSLANDS

ANTS

A GROUP OF ANTS IS CALLED AN ARMY.

You've almost definitely seen an ant. In fact, you've almost definitely seen more than one because ants love to live and travel in groups. LARGE groups. The sight of ants pouring out of an anthill looks a bit like clowns getting out of a clown car—amazing and a little bit terrifying. How do they all fit inside their seemingly small anthill? We'll get to that.

Ants are great at teamwork, they're incredible builders, and they're really good at farming, too (just wait until you hear what kind of farming—it's gross). But farmer ants don't have anything on the ants that explode, or the ones that turn into zombies . . . or vampires . . .

WHERE CAN I SEE AN ANT?

Ants have colonized every habitable continent so if a human can live there, so can an ant! The only places that ants avoid are environments that even humans find tricky to live in, like Antarctica.

MUSHROOMS AND COWBOYS

Some ants take their chances on what they'll find to eat each day, but other ants like to know where their next meal is coming from. So they farm their food!

- **Leafcutter ants** create farms underground where they carefully tend to a certain type of nutritious fungi. They even make compost for the fungi by mashing up leaves! This type of fungus doesn't grow anywhere else in the world—in fact, it can't grow without the ants' constant care. The adult ants hardly ever eat the fungus, though. They grow it just to feed to their young, and they mostly eat plant sap instead. That's dedicated parenting.

- **Rancher ants** carefully tend herds of sap-sucking aphids—tiny pear-shaped insects. They move the aphids around so they get plenty of plant sap to eat, build shelters for them so they don't get wet when it rains, and fight off aphid predators, such as ladybugs. The ants sometimes even bite off the wings of the aphids so they can't escape. **RUDE!** So why do they do all this? The aphids produce a sugary substance called "honeydew," which ants love to eat. They milk the aphids by tickling them with their antennae until the honeydew comes out . . . of the aphids' butts! That's right, the ants are essentially drinking butt-milk. **GROSS!**

SMELLING THE WAY HOME

Ants lay down trails of chemicals called "pheromones" so other ants can follow them to find food or the way home. If you want to see how important these trails are, wait for a gap between ants marching in a line, then wipe your finger through the trail. As the incoming ants reach that spot, they will become confused and turn back, or wander around trying to sniff their way back to the path.

Even though we can't smell them, the chemicals used to mark these trails are extraordinarily strong to ants. Just 1 milligram of trail pheromone can be enough to create an ant superhighway so long it could wrap around the entire world 60 times.

ANT MANSIONS

Underground ant nests are enormous—there are some the size of whale skeletons! One species of **leafcutter ant** from South America has nests that can spread over thousands of feet. These nests can have nearly 2,000 rooms in them, some of which are so big that they could fit at least six basketballs inside. The ants have to dig out almost 4 tons of earth to make a home of this size—that much dirt weighs the same as 20 rhinos!

WORKING HARD

Ants live in large groups known as "colonies." You hardly ever see an entire colony at once, but it can be the size of a large octopus! Most ants in the colony are female workers. Each colony works kind of like a human town or city, with everyone doing different jobs to keep things running smoothly. Here are just a few jobs a worker ant might have:

BABYSITTER ANTS
look after the ant eggs and baby ants, known as larvae.

EXPLORER ANTS
go out looking for food.

ZOMBIES THAT DON'T EAT BRAINS

Zombie ants are carpenter ants that have been taken over by a deadly fungus. The aim of the fungus is to infect as many ants as possible. It starts by infecting an ant's body so it can control the ant's muscles—but it leaves the brain completely intact. This is where the fungus reaches incredible levels of evil masterminding—it accesses the knowledge inside the ant's brain about where other ants hang out, then it forces the zombie ant to walk there. Then the fungus makes the ant climb up high, where the fungus can bloom out of the ant's head and drift down to land on all of the other ants below, infecting them too.

DOCTOR ANTS

nurse sick or injured ants.

TRASH COLLECTOR ANTS

clear refuse out of the nest.

... OR HARDLY WORKING?

SO IF MOST OF THE ANTS IN THE NEST ARE FEMALE WORKERS, WHO ARE THE OTHERS?

▶ **Males:** These guys only have one job—to mate with the queen. After they've finished that task they die off pretty quickly.

▶ **The queen:** The queen's only job is to lay eggs. All her needs are taken care of by worker ants. Being pampered and fussed over by hordes of dedicated servants might sound kind of cool, but there are downsides to being the top ant. In some species, once the queen begins laying eggs she never moves again, laying 20 eggs every minute for all of her decade-long life. No fresh air, no stretching of her many legs—the worker ants might have the better deal after all.

THAT ANT IS GARBAGE

Trash collector worker ants smell of garbage, and the smell makes other ants really aggressive. If a trash ant sneakily tries to do a different job, its scent gives it away—and as soon as the other ants smell it, they shove the unlucky trash ant straight back to the dump.

FRIENDLY VAMPIRES

Dracula ants get their name because they suck the blood of their larvae! That sounds pretty brutal, but don't worry— they don't harm the larvae. In fact, dracula ants carefully tend to their young just like other ants—they just take a bit of blood in return.

UNDISCOVERED ANTS

There are currently 14,000 different species of ant in the world, but because they're small and really excellent at squeezing into hidden spaces, there could be another 14,000 types of ant still waiting to be discovered. Maybe even by you!

GUNSHOT WOUND OR ANT BITE?

The biggest ant is the **bullet ant**, which lives in the tropical rainforests of South and Central America. These ants can grow up to 1 inch long—that's more than 30 times bigger than their **leptanilline** relatives. Bullet ants get their name because being stung by one feels like being shot with a bullet. The pain of their sting makes you writhe and scream, throw up and even pass out. It's the most painful sting you can get from any kind of insect, and you won't feel better quickly, either— the pain lasts for a whole 24 hours.

OUCH!

SUPER STRENGTH

Despite their size, ants are wildly strong. They can lift 50 times their body weight and still clamber over difficult terrain. Imagine being able to lift 50 of your friends up over your head and then carry them all through an obstacle course!

BURIED ALIVE!

Undertaker ants recognize dead ants by their smell, not by the fact that they're not moving. When ants die, their rotting bodies produce something called oleic acid. When undertaker ants smell this acid, they carry the ant corpse to the cemetery. If a live ant gets any oleic acid on them they are promptly carried off by the undertaker ants too, despite the fact that they are still very much alive and kicking! If they try to leave the cemetery the undertakers will just keep on dragging them back until they have cleaned off the stinky acid.

STINKY ANTS

One ant species has been given the name **odorous house ant** because when they get squished, they release a disgusting scent that some people think smells like rotting coconut or blue cheese.

GROSS!

ANCIENT ANTS

Ants used to be wasps! They first evolved into ants around 140 million years ago.

SO FRESH AND SO CLEAN

Ants' antennae are coated in tiny hairs, and these hairs need to stay clean so that the ants can communicate and find their way around. It's not hard for ants to stay looking fresh, though—they have a built-in brush and comb set on their front legs! When they brush their legs over their antennae, the bristles clear out any dust or dirt.

CLEVER!

EXPLODING ANTS

Some ants can make themselves explode to scare predators away from the colony. They swarm around the invader and cling on to them, flexing their bodies until they literally burst open. One kind of exploding ant, the *Colobopsis explodens*, releases a lethal yellow goo when they explode, making them doubly as dangerous to predators. Strangely, this goo smells pretty delicious—like curry!

SMALL BUT DEADLY

The smallest ants are **leptanilline ants**. They're less than four hundredths of an inch long, which means one of these little guys could perch on the very tip of your pen and still have space to do an ant dance. But don't let their size fool you—these miniature ants are formidable hunters. Packs of these tiny creatures swarm together to take down and devour venomous centipedes much bigger than them!

STACKABLE

Just like acrobats, **fire ants** can stack themselves into towers and pyramids to get over obstacles. Sometimes more than 30 ants stack themselves on top of each other! Huge groups can also cling together to form ant rafts that can float across water. Their feet have special, extra-sticky pads on them that help them hold on to other ants.

FENNEC FOXES

These tiny, desert-dwelling foxes are smaller than a pet cat and their comically oversized ears would look more at home on a large dog. They're distractingly cute, but once the distraction wears off you'll probably have some questions. Such as, why would anything need ears that big? And how does a fur-covered fox survive in the baking hot desert?

A GROUP OF FOXES IS CALLED A SKULK OR A LEASH.
(BUT FENNEC FOXES DON'T HAVE THEIR OWN SPECIAL GROUP NAME.)

Fennec foxes make purring sounds when they're happy.

CUTE!

WHERE CAN I SEE A FENNEC FOX?

Fennec foxes live in North Africa, including the sweleteringly hot Sahara desert.

HIGH JUMP

Fennec foxes can jump up to 2 feet high, which is about three times their height!

CLIMATE CHANGE

Fennec foxes are perfectly adapted to live in a dry, hot environment, but as global warming makes the Sahara hotter it may be difficult for even this hardy fox to cope with the heat.

ANCIENT FOXES

The earliest fox fossils are seven million years old and come from Africa. The fennec fox is a very old species of fox—its relatives have probably been living in Africa's deserts for millions of years.

AREN'T YOU HOT?

For an animal that lives in the desert, fennec foxes have amazingly lush, furry coats. Even their feet are covered in thick hair! Although it seems wildly impractical, they actually rely on their fur to survive. The sun bakes down during the day, but the desert gets unbelievably cold overnight—so fennec foxes need all that fur to stay cozy after the sun goes down. Surprisingly, it comes in useful during the day, too—without a thick covering of fur their delicate skin would get burned to a crisp in no time! The fur on their feet is especially important for getting around in the desert. If you've ever tried walking barefoot on sand on a hot day you'd know why—sand gets UNBEARABLY HOT in the sun!

NIGHT FOX

Even though they're great at keeping themselves cool, fennec foxes get uncomfortably warm if they hang out in the desert in the middle of the day. So they don't! They use their furry feet to dig underground dens where they can curl up and snooze through most of the day, heading out to prowl at night once it's cooler.

GRANDMA, WHY ARE YOUR EARS SO BIG?

The only part of a fennec fox that isn't tiny is its ears. Each ear can grow to an astounding 6 inches long, which isn't that far off the height of the entire animal. So, why ARE their ears so big? All the better to hear their prey with! Their hearing abilities are so powerful that they can pick up the sound of tiny insects moving deep underneath the sand. Once they've found the precise location by listening carefully, they can dig at exactly the right place to uncover a delicious snack. Their bat-like ears also help fennec foxes to survive in their sandy, super-hot desert homes by radiating heat away from their bodies to control their internal temperature.

ARMADILLOS

A GROUP OF ARMADILLOS IS CALLED A ROLL.

Armadillos are strange-looking creatures, with a mix of hair and armored plates covering their stocky bodies. The Spanish name for them means "little armored one" and the Aztec name translates to "turtle-rabbit."

They come in a whole range of colors, including black, red, brown, gray, yellow, and pink (read on to find out why pink armadillos are pink—it's surprisingly icky). Some armadillos can roll up into a ball, which makes them look a bit like rocks. And their vocal abilities are incredible!

WHERE CAN I SEE AN ARMADILLO?

Nearly all armadillos live in South America. Only one type, the **nine-banded armadillo**, lives in North America.

PLATING UP

Most armadillos are covered in a protective armored shell that's built out of a number of overlapping plates—a bit like old-fashioned knight's armor.

- Each type of armadillo has a different type of shell—some only have a few plates, others have more. They usually have two main plates—one over their butts and one over their shoulders, and then a number of more flexible bands in between. Some armadillos are named after how many "bands" of armor they have, like the **nine-banded** and **three-banded armadillos**.

- Most armadillos have armored sections over their tails, heads and feet, but their bellies are just soft skin. The **three-banded armadillo** is the only kind that can roll into a ball so that its entire body is protected. Armadillos that can't roll into a ball have to find other ways to protect their delicate stomachs from predators. They run and hide in their burrows when they're in danger, or dig holes to hunker down in so that only their shells are exposed.

- **Pink fairy armadillo** shells are different—they're the only armadillo whose shell is mostly separate from their bodies. It is only connected along the spine by a little bit of skin! Their shells aren't solid, so they're not very useful as armor. But they are useful for regulating body heat. There are blood vessels just underneath the shell's surface, which can take in warmth or chilliness from the air or soil. By pumping blood into their shells or draining it back into their bodies, these armadillos can control their temperature. And their shell's shade of pink can actually change depending on how much blood is oozing around near the surface!

SCREAMING
IN THE FACE OF DANGER

One type of armadillo has earned the name **screaming hairy armadillo**. You can probably guess how—it has a particularly hairy tummy and is known for the piercing shriek it lets off when it's threatened. But even if these armadillos are screaming in terror, they won't necessarily run from danger. They're actually pretty brave! Like other armadillos, these noisy creatures have been known to throw themselves on top of snakes, cutting them with the sharp edges of their armor.

FUZZY
TUMMIES

Armadillo bellies are covered with hair, and each different species has its own hairstyle. On the **pink fairy armadillo** the hair is plentiful and fluffy, while on the **screaming hairy armadillo** the hair is long and wiry. Armadillo hair is very sensitive and helps them to feel things as they move around, kind of like how a cat uses its whiskers.

GIANTS AND FAIRIES

The largest armadillos are called, appropriately enough, **giant armadillos**. They can grow to 5 feet long, which is the length of four bowling pins laid out in a row, and weigh a hefty 120 pounds. That's the same weight as eight bowling balls! The smallest armadillos are teeny tiny, and have an adorable name, too—the **pink fairy armadillos**. They can be just 3 ½ inches long, which is little enough to hold in your hand. They only weigh 3 ounces, which is a little less than two golf balls.

HIGH JUMPERS

Armadillos are known for jumping when they're startled, and it's not a small jump—they can shoot over 3 feet into the air! Seeing an armadillo jump that high would stop most predators in their tracks for a moment at least, giving the armadillo a chance to bolt away and find somewhere to hide.

BABY ARMADILLOS

Nine-banded armadillos hardly ever have just one baby at a time. In fact, they're the only mammal that regularly gives birth to identical quadruplets! Baby armadillos, called "pups," are born without the armor that their parents have. Over time, their leathery skin hardens to form the protective shell they're famous for.

KEEPING COZY

Armadillos have barely any fat on their bodies, so they can get cold really easily. They also have a low metabolic rate, which means they don't produce much of their own body heat. If it gets too cold they can die, so armadillos prefer to live in warm places. Plus, it's easier to find food in warm places, and armadillos need to eat pretty regularly when they're awake. Insects don't keep you full for long!

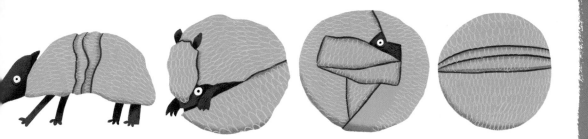

SWIMMING CHAMPS

Armadillos don't look like they could power through laps in the local pool, but they're surprisingly good swimmers! They can hold their breath for up to six minutes, which helps them walk along the bottom of rivers and streams to reach the other side. They can also swim along the surface of the water instead—if they gulp in enough air, they become buoyant enough to float near the surface as they paddle across.

SNIFFING AND SCARFING

Armadillos have an excellent sense of smell, which is very lucky because their eyesight is terrible. They rely on their noses to track down food—usually some kind of insect. They have a particular passion for ants and termites, which they latch on to with their long, flexible tongues. Their spit is extra sticky, making it tricky for insects to escape. They keep their noses buried in the soil a lot of the time, sniffing out things to eat. It's hard to breathe when your nose is full of loose soil, so sometimes they hold their breath as they dig.

I'D RATHER BE SNOOZING

Most armadillos regularly sleep for 16 hours each day, only rousing themselves in the morning, evening or at night to rustle up something to eat. The **giant armadillo** is even sleepier than the rest—it can sleep for 18 hours at a time!

TOOTHY WONDERS

Giant armadillos have up to 100 teeth crammed into their jaws.

A BUTT BUILT FOR DIGGING

Armadillos have strong paws and sharp claws that help them tunnel for their prey or build burrows to sleep in. **Pink fairy armadillos** live underground, like moles do. In fact, it's very rare to see one aboveground, as they're up and about when you're asleep. These particular armadillos have a special body part that helps them with all that digging—a butt plate! This plate is a solid patch at their rear end that they use to pat down all of the loose earth they dislodge as they dig with their paws. The butt plate pushes the loose soil to the back and compacts it, keeping a clear path ahead of them.

SCORPIONS

HOW BIG ARE THEY?

The smallest scorpion is the *Microtityus minimus*. It can be tricky to spot because it's less than half an inch long. The biggest scorpion in the world is the *Heterometrus swammerdami*. It's a massive 9 inches long, which is the width of a full-sized soccer ball (but a lot less fun to play with).

Scorpions have a reputation for living in exceptionally hot places and stinging anything that comes near them. That's not entirely correct, though. Scorpions do thrive in the desert, but did you know they can also handle freezing temperatures? And they are packed with venom, but they're more likely to go after their prey using their pincers (although that fact might not be much of a comfort!). Scorpions have a lot of other qualities that might surprise you—they love smoothies, like to take a spin on the dance floor, and do something really weird with their vomit.

A GROUP OF SCORPIONS IS CALLED A BED.

- Scorpions can't swallow solid food. Instead, they tear hunks of flesh off their prey, then vomit their stomach fluids over them. This turns the solid food into a meat smoothie.

- Scorpions can slow down their metabolism so that they can stay alive when there isn't much food around. If they have to, scorpions can survive by eating just one insect for an entire year!

- Scorpions usually try to catch their prey with their pincers instead of using the powerful stinger on the end of their tails. It might seem strange for a hunter to avoid using their strongest weapon, but scorpions don't actually have a constant supply of venom. Once the venom has been used up it can take a whole week for their bodies to make more, so it needs to be saved for special occasions. **DELICIOUS!**

GIANT SEA SCORPIONS

About 400 million years ago the ocean was home to an ancient relative of scorpions. These salty creatures were called "Eurypterids" and grew to an enormous 8 feet long—that's as long as a surfboard! Luckily for us, modern scorpions are much smaller.

CAN A SCORPION KILL YOU?

There are about 2,000 different species of scorpion and fewer than 40 of them have venom strong enough to kill a human. That doesn't mean you should go and cuddle the other 1,960 types, though! Even a non-lethal scorpion sting packs a powerful punch.

WHERE CAN I SEE A SCORPION?

Scorpions live on every continent except Antarctica.

CAN I HAVE THIS DANCE?

The average pair of scorpions waltz around together for about half an hour before they mate. If a scorpion couple REALLY love dancing they might keep tearing up the dance floor for two hours!

FLANNERY FILE

Once I was riding my motorcycle around Australia, and we stopped to camp in the outback overnight. I was sleeping on the ground because it was really hot, and a scorpion stung me. It paralyzed my arm, so I couldn't grip onto anything—which meant I couldn't ride my motorcycle! I had to get a lift to the nearest doctor, who was half a day's ride away, on the back of someone else's bike. I couldn't feel my arm for about a day, but I wasn't seriously harmed—eventually the feeling came back and I could go and pick up my abandoned bike.

SNEAKING UP ON A SCORPION

Scorpions are almost impossible to sneak up on because their senses are ridiculously sharp.

▶ Scorpions have six pairs of eyes, so they don't have a single blind spot. Their eyes can pick up on even the tiniest movements around them by tracking changes in the light.

▶ Scorpion claws are covered in tiny hairs that can sense things moving nearby. They also have a slit-shaped organ on the upper part of each leg that is so sensitive to vibration it can pinpoint the footfall of a beetle nearly 3 feet away.

▶ Scorpions have highly sensitive comb-shaped organs called "pectines" under their bodies. These organs are packed with nerve endings and are capable of smelling and tasting things from the ground as the scorpion walks.

POO FREE

Scorpions produce almost no poo—just a teeny-tiny bit of nitrogen-rich waste.

THIS SKIN IS SO LAST SEASON

Baby scorpions start out with soft skin that hardens over time. Even after they've grown up scorpions can't rely on their tough skin to protect them, because they shed the outer layer up to seven times each year. When they shuck off their old skin the skin underneath is silky-soft, so they have to lay low until it has a chance to harden into the usual armor-like coating.

HITCHING A RIDE

A baby scorpion is called a "scorpling"—which is super cute for something that can grow up to be so dangerous! Scorpion mothers carry their hordes of scorplings around on their backs like the insect versions of school buses.

CLIMATE CHANGE

Scorpions will probably survive climate change better than most living things, including us. They're very hardy and have already survived for 430 million years, making them among the most ancient of land creatures.

FLANNERY FILE

I once camped near Lake Eyre in the Australian desert. It hadn't rained for a long time, but that night we had a brief shower. When I got out of my tent and turned on my flashlight I saw that there were hundreds of transparent scorpions, about the length of my thumb, walking over the sand. There were so many it was hard to step between them. When I looked closely, I could see some of their internal organs through their skin!

PACKED WITH VENOM

The **yellow Israeli scorpion**, also known as the deathstalker, has about 100 different types of venom! Even so, its venom is rarely powerful enough to kill a healthy adult human.

ELEPHANTS

Elephants hang out in deserts, grasslands, and forests, squirting water out of their trunks, stamping around and snacking on various plants. But those aren't the only things worth knowing about them! For example, did you know that there used to be elephants the size of ponies? Or that they like playing catch? If they're feeling extra rebellious, elephants might even gang up to cause trouble for nearby hunters.

PRETTY COOL!

WHERE CAN I SEE AN ELEPHANT?

Asian elephants live in Southeast Asia, **African elephants** live across sub-Saharan Africa and **African forest elephants** live in the central and West African rainforest.

ANCIENT ELEPHANTS

Elephants once lived on every continent except Australia and Antarctica, and there used to be dozens of different species, from the pony-sized **dwarf elephants** of Crete to the huge **woolly mammoths** and **mastodons** of North and South America.

SUPER NOSES

Elephant trunks are actually noses, but they're much more versatile than a human nose. Their noses have an astounding 100,000 muscles and can do a whole lot of useful things:

▶ Elephants can drink through their trunks, but it's not like drinking through a straw. They use their trunks to pick up water, which they then squirt into their mouths.

▶ Elephants use their trunks to communicate with each other, like how humans use sign language or baseball players use hand signals to call a play.

▶ Trunks can be used like a hose and sprinkler, with elephants sucking up water and then spraying it over themselves to cool down or wash off.

▶ Elephants tear branches off trees with their trunks. Why? To use as flyswatters!

▶ Elephants' trunks are strong enough to uproot entire trees to throw at predators! But they don't just throw things to protect themselves. They often use their trunks to throw objects around for fun, like how we play catch with a ball or frisbee.

WHAT'S IN A NAME?

There are three types of elephant: **African elephant**, **African forest elephant**, and **Asian elephant**. The Asian elephant's scientific name is ***Elephas maximus***, which means "largest elephant" in Latin. That's pretty funny, because Asian elephants are actually smaller than African ones!

ELEPHANTS ARE HUGE

Elephants are the largest land animals in the world. **African elephants** can grow nearly 13 feet tall and weigh up to 24,000 pounds, and babies can weigh 220 pounds when they're born. To put that in perspective, you probably weighed about 8 pounds as a newborn!

A GROUP OF ELEPHANTS IS CALLED A HERD.

WHAT ARE TUSKS FOR?

Tusks are kind of like the elephant version of a pocketknife—they're strong, pointy and can do a whole lot of nifty things. **African elephants** have the biggest tusks.

▶ Tusks are perfect for digging up roots to eat or drilling down to reach underground water.

▶ Elephants can use their tusks to strip the bark off trees so that they can munch on it.

▶ If an elephant needs to intimidate or fight predators, or even other elephants, tusks are perfect for the job. As you can imagine, being on the other end of a pair of long tusks would be pretty terrifying!

CONSERVATION STATUS

ENDANGERED

Asian elephants are endangered and African elephants are threatened.

MOVE OVER, MICHAEL PHELPS!

Elephants are excellent swimmers. In fact, they're the best swimmer of any land mammal—except for professional human swimmers! They are able to float quite well in the water, and can also use their trunk like a snorkel and swim with their body completely submerged underwater.

CLIMATE CHANGE

Different elephant species used to breed with each other, and sharing their genes in that way helped them become stronger and more able to adapt to living in different places. Scientists worry that because the last three living elephant species no longer breed outside of their own species, they may be less adaptable and more vulnerable to climate change.

MUD BATH

Elephants love to swim in water, but they'll also wallow around very happily in a pool of mud. A mud bath helps elephants to keep cool and rid themselves of bugs. The mud has another special benefit, too—it coats their skin and helps protect them from the hot sun. Yes, even elephants can get sunburned!

FLANNERY FILE

Once I was in a bush camp in Botswana, and there was a little swimming pool there. A young elephant came right into the camp and started playing with a hose that was being used to refill the pool. The people running the camp were a bit nervous—they said an elephant had never come into their camp before. But it turned out to be harmless—and hilarious. The elephant was having so much fun! He grabbed the end of the hose out of the pool and squirted himself all over, and then started waving it around wildly and squirting everything else! I was standing a few yards away from him, so I got completely drenched.

GOT MILK?

Baby elephants survive on their mother's milk for two years. When they're being weaned they throw tantrums that rival those of the wildest two-year-old humans, screaming, trumpeting, and poking their mothers with their tiny tusks.

WAAAH!

FULL OF FEELINGS

Elephants are incredibly clever, sensitive creatures. They have excellent memories and can recognize up to 1,000 other elephants! They have been known to remove spears from wounded friends and cry when a loved one dies, just like humans do. They often bury their dead; in one case, a group of elephants broke in and raided a shed filled with the body parts of illegally slaughtered elephants, removing the ears and feet (which were destined to be turned into umbrella stands) and burying them.

RHINOCEROSES

Rhinos are big and tough, but they also have plenty of habits that are more likely to make you laugh than run away in terror—including prancing around in poo slippers and having tongues that lick like an overexcited labrador.

MONSTER RHINO

The world's biggest ever land mammal was closely related to today's rhinos. The *Indricotherium*, now extinct, is thought to have been up to 25 feet tall. It probably weighed more than 30 tons, which is the weight of eight particularly large **white rhinos** put together!

ODD RELATIVES

They don't look alike, but rhinos' nearest relatives are actually tapirs and horses!

COMM-POO-NICATION

Rhinos make all sorts of sounds when they're talking to each other, including roars, honks, bleats, grunts, and snorts. They also use their poo to communicate and mark their territory. They build huge piles of poop called "dung middens," coming back time after time to go to the toilet in the same place. **Greater one-horned rhinos** are particularly likely to do this, and their middens can be up to 3 feet high and 16 feet wide. That's longer than some small cars! After doing their business, they stomp their feet in their poo and walk their scent all through their territory, warning other rhinos to keep away. Definitely do *not* try this at home.

EW!

HOW BIG IS A RHINO?

Greater one-horned rhinos are the tallest of all the rhinos, measuring up to 6 feet from toe to shoulder—that means they'd tower over plenty of basketballers. When it comes to weight, first place goes to **white rhinos**—they can weigh up to 9,000 pounds, which is more than twice the weight of some cars. They could crush you like a bug!

A GROUP OF RHINOS IS CALLED A CRASH, OR SOMETIMES A HERD.

WHERE CAN I SEE A RHINO?

Rhinos once roamed in many parts of the world, but they now only live in a handful of places. All rhino species are under threat of extinction due to deforestation and poaching.

- The **Sumatran rhino** lives in Indonesia and Malaysia.
- The **Javan rhino** lives in Indonesia.
- The **white rhino** lives in South Africa, Botswana, Kenya, Namibia, Swaziland, Zambia, Zimbabwe, and Uganda.
- The **black rhino** lives in Kenya, Namibia, South Africa, Swaziland, Tanzania, Zimbabwe, Zambia, Botswana, and Malawi.
- The **greater one-horned rhino** lives in India and Nepal.

23

NO BABYSITTER REQUIRED

Female rhinos are called "cows," males are called "bulls," and babies are called "calves"—just like cows! Rhinos are pregnant for 15 to 16 months. Rhino moms are extremely caring and very protective of their babies, but mothering duties usually only last for two to five years. At that point the cow is ready to have another calf, so her current baby has to start taking care of itself.

FLANNERY FILE

I have touched the rarest rhino on Earth: the **Sumatran rhino**. There are only a couple left in captivity, and this one was in a zoo in Cincinnati, Ohio. It was a really big rhino, and the particularly amazing thing about it was that it was covered all over in thick, black hairs. It was very striking. The rhino seemed to appreciate being touched—it leaned into my hand a little as I stroked its flank. Meanwhile, I had this lump in my throat because it was so beautiful, and so endangered. The Sumatran rhino is the nearest relative to the **woolly rhinoceros**. I couldn't stop thinking about the woolly rhinoceros and how we've already lost it to extinction, and about how the Sumatran rhino might become extinct soon too, and then we wouldn't have any hairy rhinos anymore.

PASS THE SALT

Rhinos are big, tough vegetarians. They love to munch on soft new leaves and juicy shoots, plus stems, twigs, grasses and fruit. Rhinos consume about 110 pounds of food each day, which is like eating 110 bunches of kale (rhinos really love their greens). They don't only love plants, though—they're also mad about salt! Every few months they travel to "salt licks," which are places where salt naturally builds up. The rhinos lick at the salt with the same enthusiasm that you would eat a bag of salty potato chips.

SALT

¡RiEND OR ¡OE?

Rhinos are known for being tough, but most species only fight to protect their young or defend themselves. If there is plenty of food, water, and salt to go around, rhinos can be quite social with each other. It's usually only if resources are scarce that they start to defend their territory more aggressively (except for **black rhinos**—they have bad tempers!). African rhinos don't have incisor teeth, so they use their horns for defense, while Asian rhinos regularly use their sharp lower teeth when they feel threatened. When two animals fight, injuries can occur. Sometimes even deaths. When it comes to black rhinos, the chance of one of them dying in a fight is particularly high— about half of all males die in combat, and around a third of females. No other mammal is as likely to die in a fight with a member of its own species.

WHO'S WHO—AND HOW LONG WILL THEY BE HERE?

The name "rhinoceros" comes from the Greek words for "nose" and "horn." All species have at least one nose-horn, and some have two—those ones look particularly impressive! Tragically, their horns are prized by poachers, who often kill rhinos to take their horns. Many species of rhino are in danger of becoming extinct as a result.

- **Black rhinos** and **white rhinos** aren't actually black or white—they both have gray skin! So, how can you tell the two species apart? The most obvious difference is that black rhinos have a pointy lip that helps them pluck fruit and leaves straight from the trees. White rhino lips are much squarer in shape, which is perfect for grazing on the ground.

- **Sumatran rhinos** are one of the oldest living mammal species on Earth (which explains why they look so prehistoric). They're also critically endangered.

- **Greater one-horned rhinos** have super-long lower teeth. They can grow up to 3 inches long! They love swimming, and will often duck underneath the water to find food. They can even eat underwater!

- The **Javan rhino** has a known population of just 67, so they really need our protection.

- There are two species of white rhino: **northern** and **southern**. The **northern white rhino** is the rarest mammal on Earth. They have been killed in huge numbers for their super-long horns, which reach up to 6 feet in length. There are now only two in existence. Both are female—and neither one is fully fertile. The only hope for the survival of the species lies in new technologies that might be able to produce sperm cells from skin cells that have been taken, frozen, and kept in laboratories. The **southern white rhino** hasn't been so badly targeted by poachers, but it is still endangered.

25

NAKED MOLE RATS

Naked mole rats are one of those animals that people can't agree on. Some people think they're horrifically ugly, others find these rodents fascinating. Although they do look pretty odd—a bit like a pale, wrinkly sausage with teeth and the odd hair—their appearance isn't even the weirdest thing about them. They're one of the few cold-blooded mammals in the world, they live in colonies that are eerily similar to ants' colonies and they have some surprising uses for poo.

WHERE CAN I SEE A NAKED MOLE RAT?

Naked mole rats live in the east African desert—Somalia, Ethiopia, and East Kenya.

HOW BIG IS A NAKED MOLE RAT?

Naked mole rats are usually a little under 4 inches long and weigh 1 to 1.2 ounces, about half the weight of a tennis ball. The queen is significantly longer and heavier, generally weighing at least double any other naked mole rat in her colony and sometimes reaching nearly 3 pounds—the weight of a particularly small chihuahua.

THE SUPREME RULER

Naked mole rats live in large groups—there are usually around 75 in each colony, but there can be up to 300! Each naked mole rat has its own job within the colony, and the rules of who does what are strictly enforced. One of the riskiest things a naked mole rat can do is challenge the hierarchy of its colony. Breaking the rules is inexcusable behavior, and the punishment is often death (or exile, which for naked mole rats pretty much means death—they're not built to live alone). So, who's who in the colony?

▸ **The queen:** Naked mole rats are led by an all-powerful leader, and it's always a female. The queen is a fair bit larger than the rest of her colony, but she's not born that way; she starts out life just like all the others and has to fight her way to the top. It's her job to eat all the best food and have lots of babies.

▸ **The dads:** Not every male gets to be a father—a small handful of males in the colony are in charge of mating with the queen.

▸ **The security guards:** These naked mole rats are tasked with keeping the entire colony safe from outside threats.

▸ **The workers:** This group of naked mole rats do most of the work to keep the colony going. They dig tunnels for everyone to live in, gather food, and look after the queen's babies.

HOME SWEET HOME

Naked mole rats don't really know the meaning of the phrase "personal space"—they live packed tightly together in huge underground burrows. The burrows are a mass of winding tunnels, with separate rooms for eating, sleeping, and going to the toilet. Naked mole rats can dig closer up near the surface where the earth is heated by the sun to warm up, or deeper down if they need to cool off. Their legs are quite small and not all that strong, so they mostly use their powerful teeth for digging away at the soil, only using their feet to clear away the loose dirt. There often isn't much room to turn around in the narrow tunnels, but, luckily, naked mole rats are great at running backward!

PRECIOUS POO

Poo isn't just a waste product for naked mole rats—it is a treasured resource that they *eat*. The roots they eat are hard to digest, so by eating their poo they have a chance to get extra nutrients from their food that weren't digested the first time around.

Poo is more than a food source, too—naked mole rats roll around in the colony's communal toilet so that they all smell the same, which helps them tell outsiders apart.

BRAINWASHING THE BABYSITTER . . .
WiTH POO

Although naked mole rat colonies can have hundreds of members, only the queen has babies. All of the other females produce a special hormone that stops them from getting pregnant. The hormone only works when they're living under the rule of a queen—if any of the females leave the colony, their bodies go back to being ready to have babies very quickly. The queen has to keep on having babies each year in order to stay in power, but she doesn't take care of them all by herself—after about a month, the workers step in. They're really good at babysitting, and there's a bizarre reason for that—they eat the queen's poo, which is full of special hormones that make the workers act like mothers and take extra good care of the babies.

FOREVER YOUNG

Many small rodents don't have particularly long lifespans—take mice, which usually only live for a year or two. Naked mole rats are different, though. They can live for over 30 years, which is an incredibly long time for a rodent of their size. They usually stay fit and healthy right into old age, and they're also naturally resistant to certain diseases, such as cancer.

POOP

BREATHING IS OVERRATED

Oxygen is very scarce in naked mole rat burrows, partly because they're underground, but also because the oxygen has to be shared by everyone living there—and there are a lot of them. If you tried to move in with a colony of naked mole rats, you'd die—there simply isn't enough oxygen for humans to survive in that kind of environment. Naked mole rats are able to thrive, though, and that's due to a special skill they have—when oxygen is running low, they can stop breathing for up to 18 minutes! When they stop breathing, they keep producing energy to survive by using a substance in their bodies called fructose, which is a type of plant sugar that makes energy without using up oxygen. No other mammal has this ability. Your body uses a different kind of sugar, called glucose, which creates a lot more energy, but also uses up lots of oxygen.

TENDER OR TOUGH?

Naked mole rats live in hot, dry deserts, but they aren't bothered by their harsh climate. Despite looking delicate, naked mole rats are actually super tough. They don't feel pain the same way as other animals do—in fact, they barely notice it. When they touch hot, acidic or spicy things they don't feel the same discomfort that you would, which lets them focus on important things like finding food.

FUSSY FEEDERS

Because naked mole rats rarely leave their burrows to venture out into the dangerous world, their diet is quite limited. They eat the tubers, roots, and bulbs of certain plants that poke down into the soil, and it can take a lot of digging to find a suitable one. Naked mole rats are well suited to underground foraging. Their lips can seal behind their teeth to keep dirt out of their mouths when they're using their mouths to dig! Workers often band together to find food, lining up to dig tunnels in unison. Once they find a suitable tuber, the naked mole rats can be set for food for months, or even a year in some cases. The tubers can be very large, so even though they're being eaten by the naked mole rats, the plants often don't die. Instead, the tubers keep regrowing the parts that are being gnawed on.

HIPPOPOTAMUSES

The name "hippopotamus" comes from Ancient Greek and means "the horse of the river." Hippos certainly do love rivers—they spend about 16 hours in the water every day! However, they're not related to horses—not even a little bit. They're related to the group of aquatic animals known as cetaceans, which includes whales, porpoises, and dolphins.

A HIPPO IN THE CITY?

Prehistoric hippo bones have been found in many parts of the world, including Asia, Africa, Europe, and the Mediterranean. The bones of prehistoric hippos have even been found buried underneath Trafalgar Square in London!

WHERE CAN I SEE A HIPPO?

There are two hippo species left in the world: the **common hippo** and the **pygmy hippo**. The common hippo can be found in East Africa, south of the Sahara. The pygmy hippo lives in very restricted forested parts of West Africa.

A GROUP OF HIPPOS IS CALLED A BLOAT.

CAR CRUSHERS

Hippos are the second largest land animals in the world (elephants sneak ahead to take first place). At their largest, hippos can be over 5 feet tall from toe to shoulder and measure easily over 13 feet from snout to rump—the length of a small car. Hippos can weigh well over 9,000 pounds at their biggest—the same as more than *two* cars!

TERRITORIAL TERRORS

Hippos live in herds that are led by one dominant male. There are usually about 20 hippos in a herd, with females and babies making up most of the numbers and a couple of less dominant males rounding it out. If another alpha male invades the herd's territory, the herd leader and his sidekicks will bare their huge teeth, grunting, snorting, and splashing the water in a display of terrifying ferocity. They don't just fly off the handle at other hippos, though—any intruders, including humans, will be warned off in this way, or even attacked. So, take care to avoid hippos in the wild!

SLINGING SCAT

Hippos use their poo, also called "scat," to mark their territory. They swat their poo with their tails as it comes out, splattering it far and wide. The sound of scats being slapped echoes down the river, warning other hippos of their presence.

WHAT DOES A HIPPO EAT?

Hippos can be pretty aggressive when they're defending their territory, but their eating habits are far from brutal. Hippos like to eat grass, young plant shoots, tender leaves, and the occasional piece of fruit. Although they spend most of their daylight hours in the water, they tend not to eat water plants. When the sun sets, they take a long walk inland, munching on all the food they find along the way. Once they're full, they return as a group to their water hole. They often have to travel up to 6 miles inland to find a full meal, because their appetites are very healthy—they can eat 75 pounds of grass in just one night. In times when food is hard to find, hippos can store food in their stomachs and live off those supplies for three weeks if they have to.

EMUS

A GROUP OF EMUS iS CALLED A MOB.

Emus aren't your average birds. Their bodies are so huge and oddly shaped that their puny wings can't possibly lift them off the ground. Their stomachs are full of more than just food, the sounds they make are as far from a "tweet" as you can get, and they take the idea of dedicated parenting to a whole new level.

I AM YOUR FATHER

Mother emus leave soon after laying eggs—the fathers sit on the nest for eight weeks, keeping constant guard. They don't leave to eat, drink, or even poo, so by the time the eggs hatch the fathers are weak and very skinny. When they crack out of their shells, the chicks have downy feathers with brown and cream stripes and are small enough to cup in your hands. **CUTE!**

WHERE CAN I SEE AN EMU?

Emus only live in Australia.

WHAT IS THAT SOUND?

Emus often make grunting sounds, and they're known for hissing when they feel threatened. But the most astounding noise they make is a deep, booming call that sounds like drums being played. Emus have an inflatable pouch in their throat that they expand or deflate to make these distinctive calls. They're so loud that you can hear them more than a mile away! Females are more likely to make these thunderous sounds, especially around mating season when they're defending their territory or competing for a mate.

FLANNERY FILE

If you see an emu in the distance, lie down on your back and pretend you're riding a bicycle upside down. Emus will be so curious about the strange movements you're making that they'll come straight over to investigate. I do it whenever I'm out in the bush and see emus. It works fantastically! If you're in the opposite situation and you want an emu to *go away* instead of coming closer, there's a trick for that too. Just stand up and raise your hand above your head, with your hand curled and pointing forward in the shape of an emu's head. They'll get intimidated and go away, because you look like a taller emu!

ON THE RUN

NO TIME TO CHEW

Emu stomach acid is strong enough to dissolve just about anything they gobble down. They're mostly herbivorous, and prefer seeds and the young, tender parts of plants. Aside from super-strength stomach acid, emus have another trick to help them digest their meals. They swallow a whole heap of stones, which end up in a part of their stomach called the gizzard. These stones grind up their food, meaning emus can gulp down big mouthfuls and let the stones do the "chewing" later on.

NiFTY!

Emus don't usually stick around to tangle with predators. They can't fly away, so it's lucky they're pretty fast on the ground—they can keep pace with a car, hitting speeds of up to 30 miles per hour! Instead of running in straight, predictable lines, they zigzag wildly.

GIRAFFES

Giraffes are very relaxed animals. They like hanging out in groups, munching on leaves and taking the occasional nap. But every now and then, you'll see giraffes doing something very odd—like picking their noses or tasting pee. And things that are easy for you, like having a drink or blowing your nose, are a whole lot more awkward for giraffes!

A GROUP OF GIRAFFES IS CALLED A TOWER.

BIG-HEARTED

A giraffe's heart weighs over 24 pounds. It takes a massive heart to pump blood through their long limbs and all the way up their necks!

WHERE CAN I SEE A GIRAFFE?

Giraffes live across Africa.

STARTING A
FAMILY

- How does a male giraffe find out if a female is ready to start a family? He drinks some of her urine! By sniffing and tasting a potential mate's pee, males can work out if she's ready to have a baby, or even if she's already pregnant.

- When a baby giraffe (also known as a "calf") is born, it is much more developed than a human baby. It plops out and falls a good 5 feet down to the ground, but it doesn't get hurt—in fact, it's walking around within half an hour! Within 10 hours, it's running and keeping pace with its mom, and it's not long before it can gallop at up to 35 miles per hour.

- Mothers band together to take care of their young, forming giraffe kindergartens so that most of the parents can go out foraging while a small number stay back to keep an eye on the calves.

WHAT'S THAT SMELL?

Giraffes are particularly stinky creatures, but not because they're unclean—it's thought that the smell is a tool for keeping insects and parasites away.

TIP-TOP TONGUES

The first thing you notice about a giraffe is probably its long neck, then possibly its lanky legs. But those aren't their only oddly elongated body parts—a giraffe's tongue (which is a dark, purply black) can be over 20 inches long! That's at least five times longer than your tongue—probably even more. They need extra-long tongues so they can reach leaves from high-up branches, but they also use that extra length to reach up and lick the snot out of their own noses.

YUCK!

FLANNERY FILE

The closest living relative of the giraffe is the okapi. An inhabitant of dense African jungles, the okapi was not discovered by scientists until 1901. I once touched an okapi when I was at a zoo in America. They have much shorter necks than giraffes, but they're still big animals, and very striking. They're purple and white, and their coat is very short and unbelievably soft, like velvet. It was such a lovely feeling to be able to pat one of them!

CLIMATE CHANGE

Climate change is causing habitat loss for giraffes—flash floods and droughts kill off their food sources, forcing them to move on in search of leaves to eat. This sometimes causes fragmentation: a group breaks up, losing their safety in numbers and making it harder to reproduce. They are also affected by the drying of waterholes.

WHAT'S THAT SONG?

When you ask someone what sound a giraffe makes, chances are they have to stop and think about it—giraffes aren't known for being particularly noisy. But that doesn't mean they're silent! They moo when they're in distress and grunt or snort if startled, plus they spend a solid chunk of their evenings humming. It's thought that the humming is a way of communicating with each other, but its purpose is still a bit of a mystery to scientists.

WHAT DOES A GIRAFFE EAT?

WHAT TIME DOES A GIRAFFE GO TO BED?

Getting a solid night's sleep isn't high on the to-do list for giraffes. They generally only lie down to sleep deeply for about ten minutes per night, with a few five-minute naps sprinkled throughout the day. They don't even bother to lie down for those naps—it takes a lot of effort for such a gangly animal to lie down and then get back up. Instead, they nod off standing up—and they do it with their eyes open, too!

multivitamin—they get a big dose of calcium, phosphorus, and other minerals from gently gnawing on and licking bones.

▶ While they may be perfectly built for reaching leafy snacks from the treetops, their body shape isn't nearly so helpful when it comes to drinking. When they arrive at a water hole, giraffes need to be fairly sure there are no predators nearby, because the stance they use to drink is hard to get out of in a hurry! They splay their long legs as wide as possible, then bend their necks right down to the water so they can lap it up. Luckily, they only need to drink once every week or so—they get most of their hydration from juicy leaves.

▶ Giraffes spend most of their time eating leaves—they can eat up to 130 pounds of food per day. They don't just chew and swallow like you though—they chew, swallow, then spit their food back up before chewing it again, repeating until the leaves are a dense, gloopy lump called a "cud."

▶ Giraffes are sometimes seen licking animal carcasses. This is their equivalent to taking a

LOOOONG LEGS

A giraffe's super-long legs measure up to 6 feet—so if one of your parents stood next to a giraffe, they may not even reach its belly! Males can be up to 20 feet tall, with females generally standing a little under 16 feet. Giraffes weigh up to 5,000 pounds—that's more than a car!

LIONS

In some ways, it isn't hard to see why lions are called "kings of the jungle" (although they're actually far more likely to live in grasslands than in jungles!). The impressive mane that most males sport looks a bit like a crown—but don't underestimate lionesses just because they don't have manes! They might not be kings of the jungle, but they're certainly queens of the hunt. Despite the geographic distance, **Asiatic lions** and **African lions** aren't completely different species—these two groups are related.

BIG . . . BUT FAST

Lions are super speedy—they can race along at over 50 miles per hour, which is easily as fast as a car. They're also incredibly agile—they can launch their hefty, muscular bodies an impressive 36 feet into the air.

A GROUP OF LIONS IS CALLED A PRIDE.

WHO HUNTS?

- Male lions are protectors of the pride, while female lions are in charge of hunting.

- Lionesses love a challenge. They tend to hunt animals that are bigger than them, and sometimes faster too. In Africa, that includes zebras, antelopes, and wildebeest. In Asia, sambar deer and buffalo are some of the larger animals on the menu.

- If lionesses want the best chance of snagging a meal, they need to team up. That's why they usually hunt in packs. Sometimes they hunt alone, but usually only if something tasty wanders right past their nose—then they can't help the impulse to attack!

- Lionesses rely on their endurance to chase down their speedy prey. Once their prey is completely exhausted, the lionesses will corner it and take it down.

- **African lionesses** prefer to hunt in the evening, when the moon isn't fully out yet. They use the low visibility to their advantage, sneaking up on their prey and pouncing before it has a chance to escape.

- Lionesses are usually only about a year old when they join in on their first hunts. They tail their older relatives to learn the tips and tricks of a successful hunter.

- Not every lion in the pride gets to eat at the same time—the most powerful ones eat first and get all the best bits, with cubs being left to eat last and comb over the pickings.

THE GANG'S ALL HERE

Cats are usually quite solitary creatures, but lions are different—they live and work in tight-knit groups.

- In **African lion** prides, there are often about four times more females than males in a group—about 12 females to 3 males. Girl cubs usually stay with the same pride for their whole lives, but it isn't safe for boy cubs to stick around— the adult males in the group often see them as a threat and attack them. Once they're old enough, they usually leave and try to take over a different pride.

- Male and female **Asiatic lions** spend most of their lives in two separate prides, generally only coming together to mate.

• FLANNERY FILE •

I once had a student who was researching the first documented case of black rats in Botswana. He wanted to find out why these rats had started living in Botswana, so he went to a garbage dump to try to catch some of them for his studies. It was night-time, and all he had with him was a little flashlight and a pocket knife. He had his head down, searching, and when he finally looked up, a lioness was staring straight at him. She was only 30 feet away, so he knew that if he ran, it would be the end of him. Luckily, he remembered there was a little outhouse about 150 feet away. He figured if he could make it there, he would be safe. He backed away slowly, with the flashlight and the knife pointed at the lioness. When he got close enough to the outhouse, he turned and ran. But when he reached it, he realized it had no door—it was completely open on one side! He began screaming and shouting, but nobody could hear him. He was working with some friends, but they were back at the camp, which was about 300 feet away, and they couldn't hear him over the sound of the generator running. Finally, after a couple of hours, his friends started asking each other, "Where's Chris? He hasn't come back yet!" They went out to look for him, and eventually found him huddled up in the outhouse, looking terrified. All around the outside were the paw prints of the lioness. She'd been circling him, and had only left when his friends' car approached!

FAMILY SIZED

African lions can reach nearly 6 feet in length, plus nearly another 3 feet on top of that if you include their tails. That means that all up, they can be one and a half times as long as your bed. They can weigh up to 420 pounds, which is probably more than you and two adults combined. **Asiatic lions** are even bigger! They can weigh over 485 pounds and be as long as 9 feet from head to rump.

KEEPING CLEAN

Lions enjoy preening each other: licking each other's heads and rubbing their necks together. It's partly practical—it's impossible to lick your own head (go ahead, try it!)—but it also seems to be an affectionate gesture that helps them bond.

LIONS THROUGH HISTORY

Lions evolved from jaguar-like ancestors between two and three million years ago.

▶ Some of the world's oldest art shows pictures of lions—32,000-year-old paintings in a cave in France show lions living alongside now-extinct animals, such as mammoths and woolly rhinos.

▶ Lions used to live on every continent except for Australia, South America, and Antarctica. They lorded it up in England, France, and even Los Angeles, but now their territory is much more limited.

▶ **European cave lions** survived until 14,000 years ago. They were bigger than modern lions and lacked a mane, and some of them may have had faint stripes.

▶ **American lions** became extinct 11,000 years ago. They were the largest lions ever, with males sometimes weighing more than 1,000 pounds.

WHOSE CUB IS WHOSE?

▶ Lions can reproduce at any time of year, but females living together in the same pride regularly have babies at the same time and share the work of raising the cubs. Lionesses often babysit big groups of cubs, a bit like a cub kindergarten, and cubs will drink the milk of any mother lion in the pride—not only their mother.

▶ Baby lions are usually called "cubs," but can also be called "lionets." CUTE!

▶ If a male lion appears on the scene and tries to take over a pride, he usually kills all the cubs. Brutal! The mothers don't let that happen without a fight, though—they often band together in groups and fight back heroically to protect their cubs.

▶ Cubs are super playful. Mothers will sometimes join in with the games, but dads are more likely to get annoyed and swipe them away.

WHERE CAN I SEE A LION?

African lions live in Botswana, South Africa, Kenya, and Tanzania, with the majority grouped in a park called the Serengeti National Park in Tanzania, where they are protected from hunters.

There is just one area left in the world where **Asiatic lions** live: the Gir Forest in India, which is a wildlife sanctuary where the lions are protected and able to live in peace.

ROADRUNNERS

Roadrunners are members of the cuckoo family that have become terrestrial, meaning they spend pretty much all of their time on land. Their scientific name, *Geococcyx*, means "cuckoo of the earth" in ancient Latin. Despite being earth-bound, they can still get around! You might have seen a cartoon version stirring up a cloud of dust as it shoots across the desert, and the animated version does share some similarities with the real deal. For example, they do live in the desert, and they are incredibly fast! There are two types of roadrunner, the **greater** and the **lesser**. The greater is bigger, and has a longer bill, but otherwise they're quite similar.

ROADRUNNERS GENERALLY TRAVEL iN PAiRS RATHER THAN BiG GANGS, BUT WHEN A GROUP OF THEM GET TOGETHER THEY'RE CALLED A MARATHON OR A RACE.

WHERE CAN I SEE A ROADRUNNER?

Greater roadrunners live in Mexico and the southwestern US. **Lesser roadrunners** live in Mexico and Central America.

TRUE ♥ LOVE

Roadrunners mate for life. Some couples stick together year-round, but others go off and do their own thing for most of the year, only meeting up when it is time to mate and raise a new set of babies. When these pairs reunite there is much excitement, with special calls and dances. The male performs a mating show, parading before his mate with his head held high, then bowing right down and fanning his wings and tail out. When it's time to mate, the male will often present a dead mouse or some other gruesome offering to the female. She doesn't think it's gross, though—she's delighted!

BUILT FOR SPEED

Roadrunners have to be lightweight to move as fast as they do—the heavier ones still often only weigh about the same as a soccer ball. **Lesser roadrunners** are usually about 18 inches long and **greater roadrunners** are a little larger—more like 22 inches on average.

SOAKING UP THE SUN

Because they don't migrate for the winter, roadrunners have had to develop some clever tricks to live through the colder months. During winter nights, they lower their body temperature and become very still to preserve energy. As soon as the sun comes up, they splay out their feathers, exposing a little patch of bare skin on their back to absorb as much of the sun's heat as possible.

RAISING BABIES IS A
TEAM SPORT

ROADRUNNER PARENTS WORK TOGETHER TO RAISE THEIR YOUNG, WHICH IS RARE FOR CUCKOO SPECIES.

▶ The natural habitat of roadrunners includes dry, scrubby deserts with cactuses or shrubs for nesting in. The father goes out to hunt for building materials for the nest, and then the mother is in charge of putting it together. She cleverly weaves items such as sticks, leaves, snakeskin, and dung into a large, fairly flat nest that can reach over 16 inches wide and about 8 inches thick.

▶ Sometimes roadrunners abandon their nest after one use and build an entirely new one the next year, but sometimes they renovate instead! They mend parts that are worn and add new flourishes, so it's as good as new for the next set of eggs.

▶ It only takes about 20 days after mating for mothers to lay 2–6 smooth, white eggs. Mothers keep the eggs warm during the day, then the fathers take the night shift so their partner can stretch their legs. Parents keep this routine up until their eggs hatch, and then they keep working in shifts for another three weeks or so to take care of the newly hatched chicks.

▶ Roadrunner hatchlings aren't anything like you were as a baby—after just three weeks, they're ready to learn how to run, hunt, and fly—although they never get very good at that!

AN UNLIKELY NEIGHBOR

Roadrunners generally live in secluded desert habitats. But these plucky birds have also become increasingly used to living in suburban areas filled with humans. If you live in the same area as roadrunners, one could quite possibly pop up in your backyard!

ON THE RUN

Roadrunners can reach speeds of up to 25 miles per hour, which isn't that far off the record for human footspeed—27.8 miles per hour, set in 2009 by Usain Bolt. They have long tails that they use for braking and balancing, and they steer by tilting their tail or small wings to quickly switch direction. This is a useful tactic when running away from predators, such as coyotes.

ON THE HUNT

- You don't come across picky roadrunners; basically, if they can catch it, they'll eat it. Their diet includes frogs, snakes, lizards, centipedes, scorpions, caterpillars, beetles, crickets, and even other birds' eggs and chicks. They're one of the only predators fast enough to take on rattlesnakes.

- Roadrunners tenderize larger animals by picking them up in their beaks and thumping them against rocks or other hard surfaces. This breaks down the prey's bones and makes them a manageable meal for these fearsome birds!

- Roadrunners also nibble on seeds and such fruits as sumac and prickly pear, particularly in the winter when their preferred prey is a little harder to find.

X MARKS THE SPOT

Roadrunners have zygodactyl feet, which means two of their toes point forward and the other two point backward, creating a super cool, X-shaped footprint.

WHAT DOES A THIRSTY ROADRUNNER DRINK?

Roadrunners don't drink much water—they get most of the hydration they need from guzzling the blood of their prey. Blood is wet like water, but not nearly as refreshing—it's too salty! Luckily roadrunners have special glands in their eye sockets to ooze out the excess salt.

• FLANNERY FILE •

Once I was in Arizona, visiting a research institute, and I was really curious about the roadrunners that lived in the area. I was out walking when I saw one with a snake in its mouth, and I was so excited that I jogged toward it. The roadrunner got nervous—it dropped the snake and ran off. I was disappointed, but I went over to at least have a look at the roadrunner's abandoned meal. It turned out that the snake was actually an incredibly rare species that no one at the research institute had ever seen before! They were delighted that I had accidentally found such a rare specimen.

45

CAMELS

Whether they have one hump or two, camels are awesome-looking creatures. Their humps make a beautiful silhouette against a desert horizon, rising and falling with their strangely graceful, bobbing walk. But not everything about camels is elegant—in fact, some of the things that come out of their mouths are far from it!

WHERE CAN I SEE A CAMEL?

Dromedaries live in North Africa and the Middle East and **Bactrians** can be found in the rocky central deserts of East Asia. **Wild Bactrians** live in Northern China and Southern Mongolia. There are also lots of feral camels in the Australian desert.

ALL-WEATHER CREATURES

Camels can survive all sorts of harsh conditions that would be wildly unpleasant for you. They can deal with temperatures as low as -22 degrees Fahrenheit and as high as 122 degrees Fahrenheit.

A GROUP OF CAMELS IS SOMETIMES CALLED A CARAVAN.

THAT'S WILD!

The most common camels—**dromedaries** (with one hump) and **Bactrians** (with two humps)—aren't actually wild animals. Both species were domesticated thousands of years ago. Although plenty of these two species do live in the wild, they're descendants of domesticated animals. The only truly wild camels left on Earth are a third species: the **wild Bactrians** of Northern China and Southern Mongolia. These camels are critically endangered; there are only about a thousand remaining.

BACK OFF!

When a camel feels threatened, it spits at the source of threat—which can sometimes be a human! Their spit is combined with the contents of their stomach to make something a bit like a spit and vomit soup, and it is a very stinky concoction indeed.

THE **ULTIMATE** PACKED LUNCH

Camels travel around with something a lot like a lunchbox attached to their backs. Or in the case of **Bactrians**, two lunchboxes!

▶ The humps that stick up on camel backs aren't just decorative—they're packed full of fat. When camels eat, any extra fat gets stored away for later. The camel can metabolize the fat in its hump, deriving more than 1 gram of water for every gram of fat metabolized.

▶ When food is scarce, camels can live off the fat they saved in their humps for up to seven months!

▶ Camels hardly sweat at all, even when they're tramping around the desert in up to 122°F heat. That means they can go a lot longer without water than other big animals that sweat heavily—like horses, for example.

▶ **Dromedaries** have specially shaped red blood cells. Unlike your red blood cells, which are round, dromedaries' oval-shaped red blood cells keep their blood flowing even when they're super dehydrated.

▶ As long as there's plenty of succulent herbage around, camels don't actually need to drink—they can get enough hydration to survive just from the water in plants.

▶ When camels do find a water source, they become an incredible rehydration station, and can drink up to 30 gallons of water in 13 minutes. They can rehydrate faster than any other mammal!

▶ Once camels get to the seven-month mark without a meal, their humps start to look pretty saggy. When they get really empty, they actually flop over to the side! Once their stores of fat build up again, their humps go back to standing tall.

MEERKATS

Meerkats are really cute—they're small and fluffy, with big eyes and adorable little paws that they hold in front of their tummies when they stand up. But for something small and seemingly sweet, they can also be terrifyingly tough. You don't have anything to worry about when it comes to meerkats, but plenty of other animals do—even dangerous predators, such as snakes and scorpions, can be destroyed by a fearsome meerkat.

WHERE CAN I SEE A MEERKAT?

Meerkats live in deserts and grasslands across Africa.

How BIG IS A MEERKAT?

Meerkats weigh 2 pounds at most, so even the heaviest ones are lighter than a chihuahua! The biggest meerkats are about 1 foot long, and they can stretch a little taller when they pop up onto their back legs to survey their territory, or to let the exposed skin on their bellies soak up some sun.

ON THE ALERT

Meerkats hunt in gangs, with a small number put in charge of keeping a lookout for danger. Sentries take it in turns to keep watch for about an hour at a time. They make peeping sounds when the coast is clear; if they whistle or bark, the hunting group know they're in trouble and need to make a break for the nearest underground tunnel or find some other way to evade a predator's notice. The warning noises differ depending on whether the predator is creeping up on the ground or swooping through the sky, and there's also a whole range of sounds that let the rest of the hunting team know if the threat is minor, major or somewhere in the middle. That way, the mob can decide whether to run and hide, duck down and remain still, or form a dense group and try to look collectively intimidating.

BUILT-IN SUNGLASSES

Meerkats have big, adorable eyes with black markings around them. This marking isn't just decorative; it reduces the sun's glare so that they can keep an eye on their surroundings. They have such good eyesight that they can see things moving almost 1,000 feet away!

CLIMATE CHANGE

Climate change is making the Kalahari Desert, where many meerkats live, warmer and drier. A drier habitat makes it more difficult for meerkats to feed, grow, and reproduce.

49

SAFETY IN NUMBERS

One meerkat by itself can't do all that much damage, but a whole hissing mob of them is much more dangerous. If they gang up on something like a snake, they can frighten it away or even kill it!

SUPREME RULERS

MEERKATS ARE SOCIAL ANIMALS, WITH UP TO 50 INDIVIDUALS LIVING TOGETHER IN ONE BIG GROUP.

▶ Not all meerkat mobs are the same—just as your family is probably a bit different from the one living next door to you. Some mobs are more helpful toward each other and fight less, whereas other mobs will be more competitive and aggressive.

▶ One thing all meerkat mobs have in common is their strict hierarchical structure—a lucky few get all the perks, while the rest are forced to be hard-working (and often undernourished) underlings. It's not worth challenging the rules, though—meerkats that try to change the system can end up in a deadly fight with their rulers.

▶ Meerkat rulers often kill the babies of lowlier meerkats in the group. If that isn't brutal enough, they then either banish the parents or force them to babysit and feed the rulers' babies now that their own babies are gone.

▶ Meerkat groups might be tough, but they're not all bad. The strong cooperative group dynamic helps them to survive in a world where plenty of predators think a small, fluffy meerkat is a perfect snack.

ROOM FOR ONE MORE

Meerkats live in burrows made up of lots of little underground rooms that are connected by a network of tunnels. When they go to sleep, they stack themselves up in cozy piles. It can get chilly in the desert overnight! Meerkats don't just share their homes with each other—their burrows are also used by animals such as Cape ground squirrels and the meerkats' close relative, the yellow mongoose.

SCARY SNACKS

Meerkats eat insects, lizards, eggs, and sometimes even small birds, plus more dangerous critters such as spiders, snakes, and scorpions. They have a very clever system for eating scorpions without getting poisoned.

▶ First, they bite off the tail and spit it out. That gets rid of the venomous stinger. Then they rub the scorpion in the sand, cleaning the venom off its hard outer shell, which is called an exoskeleton. And just like that, they've transformed a deadly critter into a nutritious snack!

▶ Meerkats train their pups to eat scorpions by using a four-step process. First, they offer them dead scorpions and show them how to get rid of the poison. Second, they give them live scorpions, but make sure they've already removed the dangerous stinger. Third, they put them to the test by giving them injured scorpions to kill and clean. The fourth and final step is letting them loose on completely healthy scorpions, so they can try out their new skills.

STARTING A FAMILY

▶ In some meerkat groups, the rulers are the only ones that get to have babies.

▶ The whole gang is usually involved with rearing babies, including the mother, the father, and any siblings.

▶ Mothers don't always feed milk to their babies. This job is usually given to a babysitter—someone lower in the group's hierarchy.

▶ Meerkat pups are born with curled-up ears and closed eyes, which don't open until about two weeks after they're born. A few days later, they're allowed to leave their burrow to see the world for the first time.

▶ Sometimes meerkats that are low in the pecking order will kill the babies of the rulers (or other high-ranking meerkats) in an attempt to climb the social ladder.

DUNG BEETLES

There are thousands of dung beetle species, and they come in many different shapes and sizes. But there's one thing they all have in common—poop. They love the stuff! They're born into it, roll on it, sleep in it, dance on it, dig in it, and even eat it. It might sound gross at first, but it's actually pretty cool what a dung beetle can do with poo!

CLIMATE CHANGE

These incredible insects can help reduce greenhouse gas emissions by digging carbon-rich poo into the soil.

WHERE CAN I SEE A DUNG BEETLE?

Dung beetles live on every continent of the world, except Antarctica.

HOW BIG ARE DUNG BEETLES?

The largest dung beetle in the world feeds on elephant dung and would probably take up most of your hand, while the smallest is just a fraction of an inch long.

WHICH POO?

- Dung beetles usually prefer to eat the dung of herbivores, but certain species prefer carnivore poo. In fact, 11 different species of American dung beetle like human poo best of all!

- One type of Australian dung beetle (**Onthophagus parvus**) loves eating wombat poo. It clings to the fur near a wombat's butthole until poo comes out, then drops down to the ground to pounce on the fresh cubes of excrement. Delicious! Other dung beetles do the same thing, but they hang out near sloth or monkey butts instead.

ARE DUNG BEETLES USEFUL?

Dung beetles do a vital job when they move poo around. As they dig into the ground to bury the poo they've collected, they're doing two things: helping air get into the soil, which makes it healthier, and spreading the nutrient-rich poo through the soil instead of leaving it to harden above ground. Poo mixed through the soil is great—it helps plants to grow, which is why gardeners often use manure on their plants. Poo left on the surface of the ground isn't nearly as good—it attracts flies and other parasites, plus when it lands on plants, sunshine and fresh air can't get to them anymore.

WHO'S WHO?

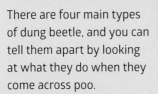

There are four main types of dung beetle, and you can tell them apart by looking at what they do when they come across poo.

❶ **Tunnellers**, also called "Paracoprids," dig their way through piles of dung and into the soil beneath it to make a burrow. They pick up bits of dung as they go, then hang out underground and snack on their poo collection (plus lay their eggs in it).

❷ **Dwellers**, also called "Endocoprids," hang out on piles of dung, eating and laying eggs.

❸ **Rollers**, also called "Telecoprids," don't hang out at a dung-pile for long. They take a chunk of the poo and roll it into a big ball, then roll it away to a quiet, safe place. They usually face backward as they roll, using their back legs to push the dung.

❹ **Dung thieves**, also called "Kleptocoprids," are tiny dung beetles that sneak around stealing dung balls that rollers have already made. RUDE!

STUBBORN STARGAZERS

Dung beetles like to move in straight lines when they're racing away with a ball of dung. Instead of detouring if they come across an obstacle, they climb up and over the object in their path. Some dung beetles use the light from the sun, moon, or Milky Way to steer straight. Every now and then they climb on top of their dung balls and do what looks like a little dance, but they're actually taking a good look at the sky so they know which way to go.

WHO ATE DINO POO?

Pieces of fossilized dinosaur poo from 70 to 80 million years ago have evidence of dung beetle tunnels inside them.

WHY POO?

Of all the favorite foods to have, poo seems like an odd choice. It's basically what's left after someone's body has digested all the good bits of their meal—so how can it be of any use to a beetle? Well, lots of animals don't actually get all of the nutrients out of their food as they digest it, especially if they eat things that are hard to break down. So there's still plenty of goodness left in their poop.

FLANNERY FILE

A number of years ago, a tiny type of dung beetle that was really good at cleaning up carnivore poo was introduced to Australia. They introduced it to the city of Sydney to clean dog poo off the streets. Once the beetles got to work, it was quite amazing. You'd be walking along, and suddenly you'd see a piece of dog poo moving on the street. The first time it happened, I thought, *What's wrong with my eyes? Surely that poo can't be moving?* But it was! There was a little dung beetle behind it, working hard to roll the poo to a bit of dirt where it could be buried. The project didn't work out in the end—I think the climate wasn't quite right for the dung beetles—but, for a while, we had moving poo on the streets of Sydney.

BORN INTO A LIFE OF POO

POO IS INVOLVED IN JUST ABOUT EVERY ASPECT OF A DUNG BEETLE'S LIFE—INCLUDING FINDING A MATE AND RAISING A FAMILY.

▶ A **roller dung beetle** male shows a female he likes her by offering her a big ball of poo. If she's interested, she often clambers on top of the ball. The male then pushes the ball, with the female riding on top, to a pleasant patch where the new couple can start their family.

▶ **Tunneler dung beetles** build their burrow before mating. The female usually does the excavating, with her future mate standing guard and fighting off any other males that try to enter the tunnel.

▶ Some species lay their eggs inside balls of poo called "brood balls" and then seal them up with their own spit and poo. The babies hatch into little grubs and eat their way out of their poo ball—it's like being born right in the middle of a big bowl of your favorite food!

ON THE HUNT

Some dung beetles, such as **Deltochilum valgum**, hunt live prey. They go after millipedes—grabbing them and biting off their heads before digging in to their feast.

HOW MUCH POO CAN YOU PUSH?

Dung beetles are stronger than any other beetle in the world. In fact, relative to their body weight, they're stronger than any other animal on the planet—including you. It might seem outrageous that a beetle is stronger than an elephant, or a rhino, or a horse, but it's true. **Onthophagus taurus**, a type of horned dung beetle, can roll more than 1,100 times its own weight in poo. No other creature on Earth can push something that weighs that much more than them!

RATTLESNAKES

Fear of snakes is pretty common, but when it comes to rattlesnakes, there's so much more to be amazed by than there is to be scared of. Sure, they make intimidating rattling noises, have incredibly fast reflexes, sharp fangs, and oodles of venom—but they don't want to hurt you! They can't eat you, so they really have no interest in biting you unless they feel threatened. Rattlesnakes are a specialized kind of viper, and they're beautiful to look at, with their colorful ridged scales and striking geometric patterns.

A GROUP OF RATTLESNAKES IS REFERRED TO AS A BED OR A KNOT.

WHERE CAN I SEE A RATTLESNAKE?

Rattlesnakes live in North and South America. The state of Arizona has the greatest number of different species.

SNAKE SCARF

The biggest rattlesnake is the **eastern diamondback**, which can weigh over 10 pounds and stretch to nearly 8 feet long. If you draped one of them across your shoulders, both ends of its body would probably reach the ground!

WARNING SIGNS

DO SNAKES LAY EGGS?

Rattlesnake babies grow inside eggs, but these eggs never get laid or hatch like chickens' eggs do. Instead, they sit inside the mother's body until the babies have hatched and are ready to come into the world. Baby rattlesnakes are born with a thin membrane around them that they have to pierce before they can feel the fresh air.

Rattlesnakes have strong venom, but they need to make sure they save plenty of it for killing their meals. If they're feeling threatened, rattlesnakes will try to warn the intruder off before resorting to biting them.

▶ Hissing is a snake's go-to tactic for telling other animals to back off. But don't bother hissing back! Snakes can't hear sounds in the air; they can only "hear" things by sensing vibrations in the ground. If you want to alert snakes to your presence as you walk through their territory, stamp your feet. It warns them that you're nearby and gives them a chance to slither off before you get close enough to frighten them.

▶ Rattlesnake tails have a number of loose pieces at the end that clatter against each other when they move. They're made of keratin—the same thing as your hair and fingernails—but they look more like bones from a human spine stacked on top of each other. They can make a clear, harsh rattling sound, or a noise like a bunch of bees buzzing furiously. Some rattlesnake species can rattle their tails more than 50 times in a single second!

57

SUPERSIZED MEALS

Rattlesnakes munch on things like mice, birds, squirrels, lizards, and even other snakes. They have a range of clever hunting techniques to capture their prey:

▶ Rattlesnakes use their sensitive tongues to taste the air around them and pick up traces of nearby food.

▶ Hunting in the dark is easy for rattlesnakes, because they have special pits underneath their eyes that are extra-sensitive to heat. These pits help them track down the warm bodies of their prey.

▶ Rattlesnakes often chase their food, but they also hunt using ambush techniques: lying in wait and striking when an unsuspecting creature wanders too close. Sometimes they keep their bodies still and gently wiggle the tips of their tails like bait to lure in prey.

▶ Many species of rattlesnake eat their food alive. They'll often paralyze it with their venom first, so it doesn't wriggle around as it goes down!

▶ Swallowing an animal whole is tiring work. Rattlesnakes generally take a few days to break down a meal inside their body, and they can go a couple of weeks between meals once they're fully grown.

DEATH BITES

▶ Rattlesnakes have sharp, hollow fangs that they use to inject venom into their prey. Their fangs are on hinges, so they can fold in and out of their mouths in the same way that a door can swing open and closed.

▶ When they're getting ready to strike, rattlesnakes harness all their power (plus look taller and more terrifying!) by raising their heads into the air and coiling their bodies like a spring.

▶ Even when they're dead, rattlesnakes can still be dangerous, because their instinct to bite doesn't stop working right away. Even hours after death, a rattlesnake can still inject venom into anything that gets too close—and its head doesn't even need to be attached to its body!

▶ Rattlesnake venom causes certain parts of the body, such as muscle and skin, to rot. It also causes internal bleeding and makes it harder for blood to clot. Bites can be very painful and need to be treated by a doctor, but are rarely fatal to humans.

FLANNERY FILE

I once had a close encounter with a particularly large snake on a research trip in Papua New Guinea. I was about to board a tiny plane to travel to a different part of the island, when some locals arrived with an enormous chest. I peered through the wire lid and saw the biggest snake I had ever laid my eyes on! It was a **Boelen's python**, which is a very rare mountain-dwelling snake. It was incredibly riled up—at one point it even struck the top of the chest, sticking its fangs right through the wire. I wanted to take the snake with me so I could study it properly, but the chest was too big to fit on the small plane. If I wanted this fierce, 10-foot-long snake, I was going to have to wrangle it into a sack instead. And it wasn't easy! The snake writhed around violently as I lifted it, wrapping its thick coils around me until my arms and legs were bound together. I thought I was done for, but luckily my friend Ken helped me bundle the snake into the sack. The pilot of the plane was *very* unimpressed when he found out what was inside the wriggling sack, but he eventually allowed us to bring it along for the ride—as long as Ken held it on his knee for the whole trip!

QUIET BABIES, NOISY ADULTS

As rattlesnakes grow, their skin gets too tight—so, just like you have to get new clothes after a growth spurt, rattlesnakes have to shuck off their old skin and grow a new one. Each time they shed a layer of skin, rattlesnakes develop a new rattling piece at the end of their tail! That's why very young rattlesnakes don't make the same sounds as their older relatives—they haven't shed any layers of skin yet, so they don't have a proper rattle. Instead, they have a little nub on the end of their tail called a "button."

WRESTLEMANIA

Male rattlesnakes go to extreme lengths to find the right mate. As well as traveling long distances, they compete with each other—often by wrestling. You might wonder how a creature without arms or legs can possibly wrestle, but rattlesnakes are masters at it! They wrap their flexible bodies around each other, squeezing and writhing around until the weaker snake is defeated and slithers off in disgrace.

MONITOR LIZARDS

You might think you haven't heard of monitors, but chances are, you're familiar with a few of them. There are heaps of different species, and they're often called by other names—like **goannas** or **komodo dragons**. These super-smart, cold-blooded lizards are remarkable in many ways! They can run, dig, swim, and climb trees —and they do all of these things exceptionally well. Add in a huge appetite and a healthy dose of venomous spit, and you've got an animal worth monitoring!

WHERE CAN I SEE A MONITOR?

Monitors are native to parts of Africa, Asia, and Australia, and some have been introduced into parts of the Americas.

A GROUP OF MONITORS IS CALLED A BANK.

ARE YOU ON THE MENU?

THERE ARE MANY TYPES OF MONITOR LIZARD, AND THEY ALL HAVE THEIR OWN OPINIONS ABOUT WHICH FOOD TASTES BEST.

- Monitor meals include anything from small spiders and insects to huge prey, such as water buffalo.

- Some monitors mix plants into their diets, but it is much more common for meat to be the focus. The **Northern Sierra Madre forest monitor** is a special exception—aside from the odd insect, it survives almost entirely on fruit!

- Monitors think snails and eggs are tasty snacks, and their strong teeth can crush the shells without any trouble. They don't bother to spit the shells out after breaking them—they swallow the whole slimy mess!

- Many monitors eat their prey whole—they have a hinge in their jaw that helps them fit even quite large animals into their mouths. When eating ridiculously big prey, monitors tear it apart and eat it in chunks.

- Cannibalism isn't unheard of for monitors. They often target monitors smaller than them, but some will even go after lizards that are bigger.

- **Komodo dragons** have enormous stomachs, and appetites to match—they can eat 80 percent of their body weight in one meal. That's why they go after oversized prey like pigs, water buffalo, goats, and deer. They can even eat humans that happen to be in the wrong place at the wrong time!

CAN I BORROW YOUR NEST?

Many monitors, like **savannah monitors**, **perenties**, and **Nile monitors**, lay their eggs right in the middle of termite mounds! The mothers dig into the mounds to lay their eggs, but they don't bother covering them back up—the termites do that part of the job. The eggs are in no danger from the termites—they're actually kept warm by all of the activity around them!

If there are no male **komodo dragons** around, females can fertilize their own eggs and they will eventually hatch into perfectly healthy baby lizards. Oddly enough, when there is no father involved, all of the babies will be born male.

TAKING A DIP

All monitors are good swimmers, even the ones that live on land. Many of them can seal their nostrils so they don't inhale water while swimming, and they can even walk along riverbeds.

I'M GOOD HERE

Ridge-tailed monitors sometimes wedge their tails into rocks when a predator is bothering them—that way they can't be moved!

HOW BIG IS A MONITOR?

The size difference between the smallest and largest monitors is more extreme than with any other group of land animals. Some of the biggest monitors are **komodo dragons**, which can stretch over 10 feet—that's nearly one and a half times the height of LeBron James! They're heavier than any other lizard on the planet, weighing up to 330 pounds. **Crocodile monitors** can actually be longer than komodo dragons—they can stretch up to 16 feet—but they're much lighter. **Pygmy monitors** are the smallest, with some species only growing to 8 inches—that's just half the height of a bowling pin. They often weigh under an ounce—not even as much as a house mouse!

FLANNERY FILE

My friend John went to a Catholic boys' school when he was little. All of the teachers, who were called "brothers," wore black robes. One of John's teachers loved to take his students on bushwalks, but he would often get lost. One day, John and his classmates were lost in the bush with this old teacher. He was standing there muttering to himself, trying to work out the way home, when a huge goanna rushed up to him, climbed up his black robes and sat on his head! The goanna must have mistaken him for a burnt tree stump. The boys weren't sure whether they should be afraid or laugh— the teacher wasn't hurt, but he must have looked completely hilarious!

READY TO RUMBLE

Monitors often stand up on their back legs to get a better look at their surroundings—but they also adopt this human-like pose to look intimidating, or to fight. When two monitors tussle, they pop up on their back legs and wrap their arms around each other in what looks like a hug. But don't be fooled! They're squeezing each other HARD. They can also wrestle and snap their jaws while wrapped in an embrace, inflicting serious injuries on each other.

SECOND-HAND
SKIN

Even though they're heaps bigger than the average reptile, monitors still shed their skin. A new layer of skin forms, and they shuck off the old one. Imagine coming across an enormous, empty sheath of monitor skin—it might be big enough for you to fit inside!

VIOLENCE, *SPEED*, MOMENTUM

Monitors are excellent hunters—their strength, speed, and tracking ability all work in their favor. Oh, and they have venomous spit.

▶ Even the smaller monitor species have remarkably powerful limbs, and the bigger species—such as the **komodo dragon**—are heavily muscled and have tails big enough to knock your feet right out from under you.

▶ Monitor tongues are forked like a snake's, and they flick them in and out of their mouths to pick up traces of their prey from the air, ground, or water.

▶ Unlike fang-sporting snakes, monitors have rows of sharp, serrated teeth that can tear through flesh and create huge wounds.

▶ All monitors have venom in their spit, but for most species it wouldn't be enough to kill a human outright—it would just cause infection and pain. Their venom works by lowering their prey's blood pressure and preventing the blood from clotting, so it streams out extra fast. The gaping wounds that monitors inflict also help the blood to spurt out more rapidly. So, when it comes to "death by monitor," although venom helps with the kill, blood loss is the ultimate cause of death.

▶ Some monitors, like **Nile monitors** and **goannas**, will occasionally work together to steal eggs from other animals' nests—including crocodiles. One monitor acts as the decoy, leading the mother away from her nest. Meanwhile, the other monitor tears into the nest. The decoy then sneaks back to join its partner-in-crime for an eggy feast.

▶ Some monitor species actively hunt their prey over long distances, but many larger species prefer to ambush their meals. The colors and patterns on their scaly skin help to camouflage them as they wait to spring out and attack.

GLOSSARY

ALPHA MALE/FEMALE

The alpha is the most powerful individual in a group of animals—the leader. There can be alpha males or alpha females, and some groups of animals are led by a pair of alphas—both male and female. Alphas usually gain leadership by fighting and defeating the former alpha.

APEX PREDATOR

Apex predators are also called alpha predators or top predators. They are on the top of the food chain, which means that they have no natural predators to fear. They play an important role in maintaining a balanced and healthy ecosystem.

AQUATIC

Aquatic animals are those that spend all or most of their time in the water.

ATMOSPHERE

Atmosphere is the gases surrounding a planet, held there by the planet's gravity. Earth's atmosphere is a very thin layer of air between the earth's surface and the edge of space.

ATROPHY

Atrophy is the wasting away or degeneration of a part of the body.

It can happen for many reasons, including the body part no longer being used or a lack of nutrition.

BACTERIA

Bacteria are microscopic single-celled organisms. They can be found in many different places: in the soil, air, and water, as well as on and inside plants and animals—including humans. Some bacteria are beneficial to us, whereas others are destructive.

BLOOD CELLS

Blood is made up of blood cells, plus a liquid element called plasma. There are three kinds of blood cells: 1. red blood cells absorb oxygen from the lungs and transport it around the body, 2. white blood cells fight against disease and infection, 3. platelets help to clot the blood and heal wounds.

CANINE

A canine is an animal belonging to the Canidae family, or dog family. This includes wolves, jackals, hyenas, coyotes, foxes, dingoes, and domestic dogs.

CANNIBALISM

Cannibalism is the act of eating a member of the same species. More

than 1,500 species are known to do this. Some species will only turn to cannibalism when other foods are scarce, but for others, scarcity has little or nothing to do with the practice of eating each other.

CARBON

Carbon is a chemical element. It is one of the building blocks that plants and animals are made from, making it essential to all life on Earth. All organic compounds are considered "carbon-based." Carbon can combine with other elements to make new compounds.

CARBON DIOXIDE

Carbon dioxide is a compound made up of one carbon atom (C) and two oxygen atoms (O_2). It is a greenhouse gas, which means it traps the sun's heat close to the earth instead of allowing it to move out into space. Too much carbon dioxide causes the earth to overheat and, as the weather changes, many plants and animals are negatively affected. This is called global warming, or climate change.

CARBON EMISSIONS

When we burn carbon-rich fossil fuels, we release a huge amount of carbon into the air. The carbon then bonds with oxygen to produce carbon dioxide. Over time, the amount of carbon in the atmosphere has risen drastically due to the increased use of fossil fuels.

CARNIVORE/ CARNIVOROUS

Carnivores are animals that exclusively or primarily eat meat—either by killing their meal or by scavenging carcasses.

CETACEANS

Cetaceans are a group of aquatic mammals that includes whales, porpoises, and dolphins. Many of them live in salt water.

COLD-BLOODED AND WARM-BLOODED ANIMALS

Warm-blooded animals, or endotherms, use their metabolism to generate the right amount of heat to keep their bodies at the right temperature. Cold-blooded animals, or ectotherms, aren't able to control their body temperature using their metabolism. On cold days, their metabolism drops along with their body temperature, which slows down their physical movement. Endotherms generally need a steady food supply to keep their metabolism generating heat, while ectotherms can often survive long periods without food, thanks to their ability to slow their bodies down and wait out the colder months.

COLONIZATION

In zoology, colonization is when animals or plants move into a new habitat and make it their home.

COLONY

In zoology, a colony is a group of animals or plants of the same kind that live together, and often rely on each other to survive.

CONTINENTS

A continent is a large landmass, and one continent often includes multiple countries. The continents of the world are Europe, Asia, Africa, North and South America, Australia, and Antarctica.

DEFORESTATION

Deforestation is the permanent destruction of forests. People clear the land to graze farmed animals such as cattle, as well as to build or to harvest wood any other tree products (such as palm oil). Deforestation causes habitat loss for many animals and can lead to the extinction of species that need the forest to survive. It also reduces the number of trees taking CO_2 out of the atmosphere, which means that our atmosphere fills up with more greenhouse gas emissions.

DOMESTICATED SPECIES

Domesticated species are animals that have been bred to benefit humans, often over many generations. Animals are often domesticated so that humans can use parts of their bodies (such as flesh, skin, fur, or bone), or things that they produce (such as milk or eggs), for food, clothing, and decoration. Animals are also often domesticated to use as labor or to keep as pets.

DROUGHT

Drought is a prolonged period with much less rainfall than usual, or no rainfall at all. Drought causes rivers and lakes to dry up, which leaves many animals without water to drink. It causes plants to die, which can result in habitat loss and less food for animals to eat. Many animal populations are threatened by drought, and climate change is increasing the instances of drought around the world.

ECOSYSTEM

An ecosystem is a finely balanced environment, in which all the living things (plants, animals and other organisms) and nonliving things (like rocks and the weather) work together to maintain the system's health.

EXOSKELETON

An exoskeleton is the hard, shell-like covering around some animals that functions to support and protect their body. All insects and crustaceans have exoskeletons; their skeleton is on the outside of their body. Some animals, such as turtles and tortoises, have both an exoskeleton (their shell) and an endoskeleton (the bones inside their bodies).

FELINE

Felines are members of the Felidae (or cat) family. They are all carnivorous mammals. Felines include lions, tigers, and domestic cats.

FERAL ANIMALS

Feral animals are domesticated animals that have been released into the wild and continued to reproduce there—for example, feral cats, goats, camels, and dogs. Feral animals can often endanger the lives of wild animals by preying on them.

FORAGING

When an animal searches for food in the wild, this is called foraging.

FOSSIL FUELS

Fossil fuels are made from fossilized plants and animals that have been buried under the soil for millions of years. Fossil fuels include things like oil, coal, and natural gas.

FUNGI

Fungi are a large group of of organisms that include mushrooms, molds, and mildews. They are more closely related to animals than they are to plants. Fungi consume organic matter to survive, breaking down dead or living organic matter into molecules that they use for energy and reproduction.

GENES

Genes are made up of DNA, and they're the things that make each animal in the world unique. They exist inside the cells of living things, like plants and animals, and are passed on from parents to their offspring. In humans, the combination of genes passed on by both parents can determine the appearance of their child, through things such as eye or hair color.

GREENHOUSE GAS EMISSIONS

Greenhouse gases absorb the heat that radiates off the earth's surface and bounce it back, trapping heat in the atmosphere rather than releasing it into space. The main greenhouse gases are water vapor, carbon dioxide, methane, and nitrous oxide. Fossil fuels are the biggest human cause of greenhouse gas emissions.

HERBIVORE/ HERBIVOROUS

Herbivores are animals that have an exclusively or primarily plant-based diet.

HIBERNATION

Hibernation is a type of deep rest that some endotherms, or warm-blooded animals, go into. Hibernation often occurs when animals don't have access to enough food or when it's too cold—certain species of animal hibernate over winter every year. During hibernation, body temperatures drop and metabolisms slow down as animals become inactive.

HIERARCHY

Hierarchy refers to a power structure within a group of animals. An alpha or an alpha pair is generally at the top of the hierarchy, with other members of the group having varying degrees of power below them. Omegas are the least powerful members of the hierarchy.

HORMONES

Hormones are chemicals inside plants and animals that help all of these living things to function. In plants, hormones help to control growth, as well as the production of flowers or fruit. In animals, hormones are used to send messages to different parts of the body to help it operate. Hormones affect all sorts of things, like growth, sleep, temperature, hunger, and much more.

HUNTING

For animals, hunting is the activity of killing and eating other animals. For humans, hunting also includes killing animals, but not always for food.

INCUBATION

Incubation is the process of keeping eggs at the right temperature while embryos grow inside them. Different animals incubate their eggs in different ways, such as sitting on them or burying them in sand, dirt, or plant matter.

INVERTEBRATE

Invertebrates lack a backbone; they either have a gooey, spongy body (like jellyfish and worms) or they have an exoskeleton (like insects and crabs).

KERATIN

Keratin is a strong, fibrous protein. It is the main substance that forms body parts like hair, nails, hoofs, horns, feathers, and the outermost layers of skin and scales.

LARVAE

Many animals begin their life as larvae before eventually growing into their adult form. Larvae generally look completely different from their parents, and often need very different conditions to survive. For example, tadpoles are the larvae of frogs, and caterpillars are the larvae of butterflies.

MAMMALS

Mammals are a very broad class of animals. Some walk, some swim, and some fly, and their diets can vary from carnivorous to herbivorous, but they all have a number of traits in common, including that they have hair or fur, feed their young with milk, and are warm-blooded.

MARSUPIALS

Marsupials are a group of mammals. Most female marsupials have a pouch where they keep their babies when they're very young, so that they can continue to grow and develop in a safe, warm place. Some marsupial species are herbivores, others are carnivores, and there are also some omnivorous species. Most of the world's marsupials live in Australia and South America.

MEGAFAUNA

The word "megafauna" means "giant animal." It is most commonly used to refer to animals from the Pleistocene epoch (the end of the last ice age), which are the larger ancestors of animals alive today. However, species that are alive today can also be referred to as megafauna —common examples include elephants, rhinos, hippos, giraffes, lions, bears, and whales.

MEMBRANES

A membrane is a thin layer of tissue. Membranes can be found inside all living things—each cell inside a plant or animal is surrounded by a membrane—but membranes can also be found in many other places. Some animals are born completely surrounded by a membrane, which they then break out of, and other animals have protective membranes underneath their eyelids that help keep their eyes safe.

METABOLISM

Metabolism refers to the chemical reactions that happen inside an organism to keep it alive. There are many different metabolic reactions, but the main ones involve releasing energy or using energy. For example, an animal's metabolism digests the food it eats and converts that food into a form that can be released as energy. Animals also use their energy to grow and repair their bodies.

MIGRATION

Migration is a movement from one place to another. Animals often migrate each year at about the same time, and different species migrate for different reasons. Migrations commonly occur as animals travel to places where food is more plentiful, or the weather is better, or to places where they can find a mate or breed.

NOCTURNAL

Nocturnal animals are active during the night and rest during the day.

OMNIVORE/OMNIVOROUS

Omnivores are animals that eat a variety of meat and plant matter.

ORGANISM

An organism is an animal, a plant or a single-celled life form.

OXYGEN

Oxygen is a gas that makes up part of the air we breathe. It's highly reactive, which means it bonds easily with other elements (for example, carbon). Animals rely on oxygen to survive—they breathe it in and use it to convert nutrients into energy, releasing carbon dioxide as a waste product of this process. Plants exist in perfect symbiosis with animals, as they absorb carbon dioxide and release oxygen.

PARASITE

A parasite is an organism that makes its home in or on an organism of another species, relying on it for food, shelter, and everything else it needs to live. The organism that a parasite makes its home on is called its "host."

PECTINES

Pectines are comb-like structures found on many animals. They can be used for many different things, including grooming, filtering food,

and as a sense organ to help the animals feel their surroundings.

PHEROMONES

Pheromones are a type of hormone—a chemical that some animals release to communicate with other members of their species. Pheromones can be released for many reasons, including to attract a mate, to mark pathways leading to home or food, and even as a warning sign.

PIGMENT

Pigments are colored chemicals in the tissues of animals. Some animals produce their own pigments, whereas others get them from their food.

POACHING

Animal poaching is the illegal capturing or killing of animals.

POLLINATION

Pollination is the way that plants reproduce to create seeds and fruits. Pollination involves the movement of pollen from the male part of a flower (the anther) to the female part (the stigma). Some plants self-pollinate, meaning that the transfer of pollen happens within a single flower, or between different flowers on the same plant. The other form of pollination is cross-pollination, where pollen travels between different plants. Things like wind and water can help pollen to travel between plants, but many plants rely on "pollinators"— animals such as birds and insects— to transfer their pollen.

POLLUTION

Pollution is the introduction of harmful materials or substances into our environment. The three main types of pollution are water, air, and land pollution. Some examples of pollutants are microplastics in the ocean, greenhouse gas emissions in the atmosphere, and pesticides used in agriculture.

PREDATOR

In zoology, "predator" usually refers to an animal that hunts other animals for food. Parasites are also a kind of predator. Predators are essential to a balanced ecosystem.

PROBOSCIS

A proboscis is a long, flexible snout or feeding organ. Many insects use a proboscis to eat, like some moths and butterflies, but larger animal species can also have a proboscis— like elephants and solenodons.

SANCTUARY

A wildlife sanctuary is a carefully designed environment where endangered wild species are brought to live and be protected from human threats, such as poaching. Proper sanctuaries are as much like the animals' natural habitats as possible: they have the right climate, and contain the right variety of plant and animal species.

TERRESTRIAL

Terrestrial animals are those that spend all or most of their time on land.

TERRITORY

An animal's territory is the area of land or water that it lives in, claims as its own and defends against trespassers.

TIDE

The tide is the periodic rise and fall of the ocean. Changes in the tide are caused by the earth spinning around, and by the gravitational pull of the sun and the moon.

VERTEBRATE

Vertebrates are animals that have a spine and a well-developed skeleton inside their bodies.

WILD SPECIES

Wild species are animals that have evolved without human interference and live and reproduce independently from humans.

INDEX

ACKNOWLEDGMENTS

I'd like to thank Jane Novak for suggesting this project to me, and the fantastic team at Hardie Grant Egmont, especially Ella Meave. Without their dedication, this book would never have seen the light of day. I'd also like to thank Sam Caldwell for his brilliant illustrations, and Pooja Desai and Kristy Lund-White for their magnificent design work. I owe much gratitude to my wife Kate Holden and our son Coleby. They put up with long absences as I wrote this book. Many colleagues helped me with information, among whom Kris Helgen and Luigi Boitani deserve special mention.